D0389473

How to Understand the Bible

TO THE STUDENTS:

The fact that this volume is being used as a text or reference in Northland Baptist Bible Institute does not mean that the Institute endorses its contents from the standpoint of morals, philosophy, theology, or scientific hypotheses. The position of Northland Baptist Bible Institute on these subjects is well known.

In order to standardize the work and validate the credits of the Institute, it is sometimes necessary to use books whose contents the Institute cannot wholly endorse because no entirely satisfactory publication is available.

NORTHLAND BAPTIST
BIBLE INSTITUTE

Dunbar, Wisconsin

How to Understand the Bible

Ralph Herring, Frank Stagg, and Others

Broadman Press
Nashville, Tennessee

1573

To the Memory of
Ralph A. Herring
Bible scholar, beloved pastor,
denominational leader,
and Christian gentleman
this book is affectionately dedicated.

Library of Congress Catalog Card Number: 74-75674
Dewey Decimal Classification: 220.07
Printed in the United States of America

Preface

This book is the fulfillment of a dream. In God's divine plan, the person who had that dream and did much of the work toward its fulfillment passed on to his eternal reward before his dream and the ensuing manuscript found expression in these pages.

That person was the late Ralph A. Herring. While serving as director of the Seminary Extension Department, Dr. Herring envisioned a Seminary Extension course which would interpret the true meaning of the Bible and some of the ways God communicated and communicates his divine message to us. Dr. Herring developed an outline for this book, enlisted and made assignments to writers, and did preliminary editing on the manuscripts when they were submitted by the contributing authors.

Although he planned for the book to be used as a text for a Seminary Extension course, as indeed it is being used, he hoped that it would have a wider usage in the Christian community. The Seminary Extension Department is happy, therefore, to cooperate with Broadman Press in making this book available to all who are interested in benefiting from it.

In a real sense, this book, which combines sound scholarship and deep commitment to God and his Word, is a reflection of Dr. Herring's life. Although an outstanding Bible scholar, beloved pastor, and prominent denominational leader, Ralph A. Herring was first and foremost a devout Christian.

Raymond M. Rigdon
Director
Seminary Extension Department

Foreword

Throughout their traceable history Baptists have affirmed the Bible to be their authoritative rule for faith and practice. They have refused to bind themselves to or by any creedal formulation, contending for the freedom of individual conscience before God. Put another way, they have contended for an open mind before the open Bible in the never-ending quest to know the mind and will of God for his people.

It is true that Baptists have drawn up various confessions of faith (cf. among others the London Confession in 1644, The Philadelphia Confession in 1742, and The New Hampshire Confession in 1833); and various Baptist institutions have drawn up their own abstracts of principles. The Southern Baptist Convention has formulated statements of faith, both in 1925 and 1963. But Baptists have held Scripture itself to be above all such creeds and abstracts. These creeds and abstracts intend to draw upon and integrate the intention of Scripture, not to displace or supersede Scripture.

The editors and contributors of this book offer it as a guide to the study of the Bible, not as a substitute for the Bible. We hold the Bible to be divinely inspired and authoritative for faith and practice. We believe that God created the world and that he made man unique in all his creation, having created man in his own image. Whatever else this means, it means that God and man are sufficiently alike to enable them to communicate with one another. God can make himself known to man and understandable to man. He reveals something of himself in all that he does, and his fullest self-revelation came in Jesus Christ, Immanuel (God with us), the Word made flesh. The Old Testament is basically the prophetic witness to mighty acts of God in creation, in delivering his people, as from Egyptian bondage, and in the formation of Israel as his own people. The New Testament is basically the apostolic witness to the continuing acts of God, cul-minating in Jesus Christ.

Initiative belongs always to God, in creation, revelation, and re-demption; but it is also important to see that in revealing himself to man and in saving man, God does not override the personhood of man. He never reduces man to a thing, a mere object to be manipu-lated. He speaks to the mind and conscience of man, eliciting a genuinely human response. Applied to the Bible, this means that it is both a divine and a human book. It is divine in that ultimately it comes from God. It is human in that it comes through man. As Scripture itself declares, "Not by the will of man was prophecy borne at any time, but being borne along by the Holy Spirit, men spoke from God" (2 Pet. 1:21, author's translation). This clearly affirms divine inspiration. It also recognizes that men did the writing. They were moved by the Holy Spirit, but their humanity was preserved as they wrote. The Bible never claims that it fell from the sky un-touched by the hands of man. The Koran and the Book of Mormon make such claims for themselves, denying that man shared in their production, but the Bible would reject this. It belongs to the glory and relevance of the Bible that God did not bypass man in giving us the Bible. Here as everywhere, he works in, through, and within man.

The Bible then is God's inspired and authoritative word to man. It is also his gift to us through inspired men. The Bible is God's book. It also bears the "fingerprints" of the men God chose through whom to speak to us. That is why we may read it with confidence as authoritative for faith and practice. That also is why we must study the life situations out of which the various writings come, the languages in which Scripture was written, and utilize all possible helps in under-standing the intention of Scripture.

Frank Stagg, Professor
New Testament Interpretation
Southern Baptist Theological Seminary
Louisville, Kentucky

Contents

1.
The Book of Life
Eugene A. Nida

Discouraged, out of work, and despairing of the future, Juan trudged out toward the dump heaps of Oruro, Bolivia, kicking up the salt-encrusted dirt as he walked along. Juan had been a labor agitator in one of the mining companies, trying to get justice for the workers. Now he was hungry, tired, and angry, both with society in general and with his own lot in particular. Suddenly his foot struck something. Looking down, he saw some pages, part of a book. There were no covers. Most of the pages were badly stained, but they were still legible. Reaching down, he picked up this coverless book, brushed off the dirt, and started to read: "Vanity of vanities! All is vanity. What does a man gain by all the toil at which he toils under the sun?"

These words spoke with biting relevance to Juan, and he was amazed at what he read. He noticed that he was reading from about page 500. He wondered what could have preceded this timely statement; so, he decided to sit down right there and read on. At chapter 4 he read of "all the oppressions that are practiced under the sun" and "the tears of the oppressed . . ., with no one to comfort them."

In all his life Juan had never read a book with such startling up-to-dateness. Even though the language seemed rather old-fashioned, the ideas certainly were not.

But shortly this part of the book was finished. Now he began to read a love story with bold and sensuous figures of speech depicting human love in passionate and beautiful ways—without the least bit of sordid, crude language so typical of the cheap novels sold at newsstands.

So impressed was Juan with this book that he determined to read it all—mostly by the light of a feeble street lamp not far outside the small window of a garret room which he shared with a couple of friends. The writings of Isaiah were difficult to understand, but Jeremiah was "tremendous." In fact, Juan declared to his friends that this man should be the patron saint of the labor agitators. He was a person who was constantly in trouble for denouncing kings, princes, and the rich. Juan discovered that Jeremiah often had to stay in hiding because he dared to speak out against the trickery and deceit of the ruling class. Once, in a time of crisis, the ruling class freed the slaves to get their support, then quickly enslaved them again after the danger had passed. Juan was also impressed with the shepherd called Amos.

Finally, he came to a blank page, except for the words "The New Will" (or "Testament")—something which he did not understand. Then began a fascinating story by Saint Matthew about Jesus Christ, whom Juan had always thought of merely as a crucifix in the church. Most important of all was that sermon of Jesus in chapters 5 through 7. "Man! That is better than the Communist Manifesto," Juan exclaimed to his friends. "This would not only change society, it would change people, if only we could get men to practice it."

After the story of the death and resurrection of Jesus the book abruptly stopped—except for a few pages written by Saint Mark, whose words seem to be very similar to what Juan had already read.

For several days Juan did little else than read and reread this unusual book. Finally, realizing that there was no point in staying on in Oruro, where he was on the blacklist with employers, he decided to return home to Cochabamba. Furthermore, he could not live off his friends any longer. So getting together what few possessions he had, he borrowed enough money to buy a ticket on the rickety old train. He set off carrying the pages of his newly found book carefully wrapped in heavy paper.

While going through the crowded train to find a seat, Juan ran across an old school chum whom he had known years before in Cochabamba. Immediately they found a place to sit together. Before long Juan had to share his experience of this strange book. As he glowingly related its incredible contents, his friend looked puzzled and perplexed. At last he exclaimed, "But Juan, don't you know that is a Bible?" "Impossible!" Juan remonstrated. "You know I wouldn't have anything to do with the priests, the church, or anything associated with Christianity." "Nevertheless, what you have is part of the Bible," his friend insisted. Then he began to explain how he himself had become a believer, a so-called "evangelical." Moreover, he had a complete Bible with him, and by comparing the two, Juan was able to see just what those pages of his really were.

Not long after this Juan himself became a Christian. It was in the Baptist church of Cochabamba, that I had the opportunity of talking with him—still an agitator—only this time, an agitator for God.

The Bible in the Modern World

This experience of Juan's illustrates how the Bible speaks to the dynamic and revolutionary times in which we live. It is true that in the twentieth century the Bible is often dismissed as strictly pre-scientific, an archaic "hangover" from a pastoral age, having little to say to us today. Actually, however, the Bible is the most universally understandable and comprehensible document which has even been produced. It came from that part of the ancient Fertile Crescent through which passed more cultural influences, and out of which spread more patterns of life and thought than has been true of any other area in the history of the world. If there is any special cultural problem in comprehending the Scriptures, the difficulty lies with modern Western man, who belongs to the "aberrant technological society." To him the Bible may seem strange, but he has more resources than any other man ever had for understanding the background and setting of former times. When modern man approaches the Bible without his prejudices, as Juan did, he finds its message strangely contemporary.

Even though some persons insist that the Bible is incomprehensible and even that God is dead, there is an almost unbelievable demand for the Scriptures in meaningful language. Within a three-year period (1964-1966) the total distribution of the Scriptures (Bibles, New Testaments, portions, and selections) throughout the world almost tripled—nearly one hundred million copies a year. Moreover, this demand for the Scriptures represents interest not only among Protestants, who have traditionally encouraged the translation, distribution, and reading of the Bible, but also more recently among the Roman Catholic and Orthodox churches which have experienced important movements of biblical renewal.

One may reasonably ask just why there should be such an increased demand for and interest in the Bible. Is this merely a coincidence, an accident of our times? No indeed! There are very important reasons why the Bible is speaking to so many modern people with increased significance.

In the first place, the Scriptures are admirably designed to speak with startling frankness to our present "Age of Disillusionment." Men have despaired of human insitutions. In a kind of refreshing and radical honesty they have stripped off the masks of certain favorite idols and exposed precisely how some institutions function. Many people look on churches as status symbols; service clubs as instruments of personal advancement; organized charity as profitable business; and ever-higher living standards as excuses for conspicuous consumption. But in the midst of such radical cynicism about modern life, man is nevertheless courageously hopeful. He lives on the brink either of total destruction or of a new world in which technology (for the first time in the history of the world) may be able to relieve hunger and suffering. It is a time when even mutual fear may provide the cement for a new structure of international peace.

Hence, to modern man, who is so skeptical about human nature and yet so hopeful that the light may yet shine in the present darkness, the Bible comes with a startlingly timely message. If the Bible is fundamentally pessimistic about what man is ("there is none righteous, no not one"), it is equally insistent about what man can be, by the grace of God ("to all those who received him, who believed on his name, he gave the power to become the children of God"). Such radical pessimism combined with infinite hope strikes a sympathetic chord in the thinking of modern man.

The Scriptures also speak to contemporary man because of their unique view of history. In contrast with the Orient's cyclical interpretation (history is viewed as always returning to the same point, merely to repeat itself), or the concept of the "beaten path" (people go on living in the same old way merely because their ancestors did), or the ideal of the "Golden Age" (people look back to some prior time, when they imagine that all was immeasurably superior), the Bible presents a concept of history in which man looks forward to the goal of God's will being done upon earth, even as it is in heaven. This dedication of life to ultimate and meaningful goals of humanitarian and God-honoring service is unique in the religions of the world. Hinduism and Buddhism provide meaning only in terms of ultimate escape from the world and loss of individuality in the world soul or Nirvana. Other religions may offer heavenly rewards or earthly triumphs. But none provides a picture of ultimate meaning in the here and now—"a kingdom" toward which both man and God work.

The Bible is especially a singular book in view of the incomparable personality of Jesus Christ, who is its central theme. Consider him who was so evidently man and at the same time so obviously God; who demonstrated such startling power and at the same time such convincing humility; who was the very center of all men's attention but who consistently and continually turned men's attention from himself to God—a miracle worker who was never theatrical, a teacher who was never professorial, a master who never insisted upon his rights, and a healer who never made gain out of his patients. It is no wonder that after almost two thousand years this God-man continues to be history's most attractive, disputed, beloved person.

Likewise, the Bible brings modern ideologies up short by its claim that love is the most powerful influence in the world—"love your enemies," "love one another," "love your neighbor." The Bible not only teaches this kind of love but also demonstrates it in action in the person of Jesus Christ. Various socio-political systems have based their hopes on force, education, social conditioning, and mass communication. Nevertheless, none of them have been so bold as to claim and to demonstrate that love is the one power which can radically change the character of man. A young man once dashed into the offices of the Bible Society in Minneapolis. In a demanding tone of voice he asked for a list of Protestant beliefs. "I have a Protestant girl friend," he explained. "I want to prove that she is wrong on every count." After talking with staff members awhile he was convinced that perhaps the best way to understand what Protestants believe would be to obtain a New Testament and to read it. Some months later he returned—a very different young man. Wistfully he said, "Whenever I read that book, someone seemed to keep speaking to me." Then he added, "I never dreamed that anyone could love like that man Jesus."

The "constraining love of Christ" is the one overwhelming power so vividly revealed in the Scriptures. And this Jesus is the eternal Contemporary who "keeps speaking" to modern man.

Methods for Grasping the Significance of the Scriptures

It is one thing to realize that the written Word has incredible power to change life. It is quite another thing to understand how this transforming power of the living Word may be grasped.

Meaningful Translations

In the first place, the Scriptures can only speak to one if they are translated into the language of life. The words must come directly from the lives of people and speak with relevance to everyday situations. This means that many figures of speech in the Bible cannot be translated literally. They need to be translated to accommodate our understanding of them. For example, in Genesis 3:8 the Hebrew text speaks literally of the "wind of the day." This is generally translated as "evening" or "cool of the day." In the Middle East it is only after the sun goes down and the evening breezes begin to blow that one can speak of the "cool of the day." Some expressions are quite meaningless to most English speakers, for example "gird up the loins of your mind" or "circumcision of the hearts." Others seem unduly quaint, such as "give ear to his voice," "there was evening, there was morning, one day." Still others were syntactically very awkward, for instance "unto the praise of the glory of his grace" and "grace and apostleship to bring about obedience to the faith for the sake of his name among all the nations."

If, however, the Word of life is to be an instrument for a new kind of life—the "eternal life" of the Bible—people must be able to understand it. The Scriptures must be translated meaningfully into all the languages of the world, some of which contrast radically with Greek and Hebrew in linguistic structures and cultural backgrounds. Therefore, although the message is the same, it is inevitable that the forms of expression will be diverse.

Translations of the Bible should communicate to each generation in such a way that the message will have the same relevance for life, will produce the same dynamic response as it did for its first hearers. Because languages change so rapidly, it is essential that new translations and revisions be prepared periodically. The message of life should not be proclaimed in words which seem to belong to a dead generation.

Indeed, we often bind the Bible in "funereal" black and treat it more like a religious relic of a bygone age than as the living book it is. Actually, the language of our most familiar English translations seem archaic and ecclesiastical in tone. For this reason new readers of the Bible may get far more out of such New Testament translations as Phillips' *The New Testament in Modern English, The New English Bible,* or *Today's English Version* which is called Good News for

Modern Man. (This last translation has been especially prepared by the American Bible Society for new readers of the Holy Scriptures and has had an amazing response.)

Effective Bible Reading

Nevertheless, translating the Bible into contemporary language is not the only important means for enabling people to grasp the significance of the message. People must also learn how to read the Bible. To comprehend the real meaning of the Word of God, however, it is not enough to read the "precious promises" and to dwell on a select number of "favorite passages." One never fully appreciates the Bible unless he reads whole chunks of it and studies the overall thrust and purpose of its message. The Scriptures may otherwise become a gimmick to prove outlandish theories or to justify all sorts of pet sins.

Because of the Bible's diversity of circumstances and content, some introductory explanations or guides to reading are almost indispensable. One may start off with Genesis and bog down in Leviticus unless he is highly motivated. In reading the Old Testament it is important to get the bird's-eye view as well as the scholar's appreciation for detail. Man's constantly recurring and seemingly innate rebellion against God forms the background to the successions of judges, prophets, and kings. Similarly, to appreciate fully a Gospel such as Matthew or John, one should read a whole book at a single sitting. Only then does he come to appreciate the dramatic sequences, the overall structure, and the interplay between related parts.

Radical Obedience

Though some persons read the Bible extensively, they seem to be quite adept in overlooking those elements in the message which are the most relevant and applicable to themselves. This does not mean that they reject what is favorable to them. Not at all! Rather, they suffer "momentary lapses of consciousness" when they come across something that is hard to take. They develop blind spots. For example, in the accounts of ancient Israel, they seemingly see no parallels between their own failures and the sins denounced by the prophets—national pride, oppression of the poor, false weights and measures, and the sexual degeneracy in fertility cults. The tendency for ancient Israel to depend upon Egypt's horses and chariots is strikingly parallel to our own dependence upon force of arms rather than upon the power of righteousness. Too often people read Ecclesiastes without ever wrestling with the real problems which "the Preacher" poses. They think of Job only in terms of his final rewards, giving little attention to the profound questions which he raises and the hopelessly inadequate answers which his friends—and we—so often give.

We are all adept at screening out what we do not want to hear. This is no excuse for gliding over the "hard words" of Jesus: "If any one strikes you on the right cheek, turn to him the other also" (Matt. 5:39). "If you do not forgive men their trespasses, neither will your Father forgive your trespasses" (Matt. 6:15). "All who take the sword will perish by the sword" (Matt. 26:52). "Woe to you, when all men speak well of you, for so their fathers did to the false prophets" (Luke 6:26). "If they persecuted me they will persecute you" (John 15:20).

To read the Bible correctly means putting it into practice, accepting it for the totality of life. Otherwise, our reading of it is mere sounding brass and clanging cymbals. We have really not read the Bible if it does not influence our attitudes. The spiritual issue is not how much we give but how much we keep for ourselves, how we invest our funds (to make a profit or to help build a better world), how we make out an expense account. It is concerned with the use of our bodies, not the abuse of them (whether with alcohol, tobacco, or overeating). It is a matter of doing an honest day's work, not cheating on coffee breaks or loafing on the job. It concerns our attitude toward sex—whether it is a beautiful experience of mutual giving or a crude demonstration of selfish getting. It is a matter of helping others or expecting to be helped.

A Revolutionary Power in History

Many of us who are familar with the Bible have never fully comprehended how utterly revolutionary it is. It proclaims a message which is designed to produce total world revolution—not by killing but by being killed; not by causing others to suffer but by a willingness to suffer. This, of course, is precisely the meaning of Calvary. Jesus said, "If any man would come after me, let him deny himself and take up his cross and follow me" (Mark 8:34, RSV).

Sometimes those who have come to the New Testament for the first time exhibit more insight as to its radical, revolutionary character than do those who are often immunized to its message. Some time ago in Thailand, copies of the New Testament were being offered to Buddhist monks in various temples in Bangkok. Most of the monks accepted the New Testaments both with interest and appreciation. They were curious about the story of Jesus Christ and the history of the Church. In one temple, however, the monks refused to receive the New Testaments. "Our abbot has warned us," they said. "He himself reads the New Testament but he said that we should never read it unless we were prepared to lose sleep." Unfortunately, too many Christians make a habit of reading the Bible to put them asleep!

Wherever there has been honest encounter with the truth of the Bible, the power of God has been manifested. This is what happened in the Valley of Tasquillo, some hundred miles north of Mexico City, where in one of the most poverty stricken and fanatical regions of Mexico, a small band of believers has grown within the last ten years to a community of more than twenty churches, scattered through the barren hills of this semidesert region.

This did not take place without the martyrdom of several of the believers and the persecution of many more, but despite and in some measure because of such tests of faith this community of believers has developed a radiant vital faith, summarized so neatly by the leader, Venancio Hernandez, as "redemption." He explained, "This means first the redemption of our hands." Then he described the new hand industries which had been introduced; the new farm which members of the church had bought cooperatively; and the new road into a nearby valley. The road had been built with pick and shovel in order to alleviate the dire poverty of people who had to carry produce out on their backs.

But redemption also means "redemption of our minds," Venancio insisted. The church had instituted classes so that adults could learn to read, and there was a rule that anyone who had acquired a trade or skill was under obligation to teach it to anyone else who wanted to learn. As a result, this Christian community included an unusually high proportion of persons who were skilled mechanics and artisans.

These people also believed in "redemption of their bodies," for divine healing was an important part of their dependence upon God. Often these people had neither the money nor the opportunity to obtain adequate medical help, and they had experienced important and convincing answers to their prayers for healing of their bodies.

This did not, however, prevent them from encouraging some of their young people to train as nurses or from putting an adequate sewage system in their town.

Finally, Venancio said, "We believe in redemption of our souls of our whole being." In essence this explains the dramatic effects which this movement of the Spirit of God has had in the Valley of Tasquillo. True worship, characterized by exuberant joy and real faith, has been accompanied by a transformation in living standards and in peaceful relations between otherwise hostile, quarreling, and fighting communities.

But what happened in the Valley of Tasquillo in Mexico is by no means unique. This is precisely what has been happening for nearly two thousand years—whenever and wherever men have been confronted with the Scriptures. In fact, the capacity to produce important and radical change has been the distinctive element in the history of the Bible.

Two centuries before the time of Christ the Old Testament was translated into Greek and had a marked effect upon many people in the ancient world. They were much impressed with the Bible's distinctive teaching about God and with its radically different concepts of justice and mercy. Though most of these persons did not themselves become Jewish proselytes, many did become the devout "God-fearers" among the Gentiles. One of these God-fearers was Cornelius, the centurion whose story is recorded in Acts 10.

For the early Church it seemed only natural that the Holy Scriptures should be translated into the languages of the ancient world. But when the printing press was invented 500 years ago, the Bible had been translated into only 33 languages. It is even more amazing that when the Bible Society movement was founded about 150 years ago, the Bible had been translated into only 72 languages. During the nineteenth century, however, rapid progress was made. The Bible or at least some portion of it was translated into over 450 languages. During the first half of the twentieth century 500 other languages were added to the list. By 1966 at least some part of the Bible had been published in 1,250 languages (237 have the whole Bible and 297 others have the complete New Testament).

But the power of the message of the Bible is not reckoned merely in terms of the number of languages into which it has been translated, or of the extent of its circulation. Its power is evidenced in the impact which its message has had upon the lives of people and nations. Beginning with the sixteenth century, there have been four principal movements directly related to the Bible.

In the first place, it was the availability of the Scriptures, first in Greek and Latin and then in many of the vernaculars of Western Europe, which played a very crucial role in the Reformation. In turn, it was the Reformation which created a strong demand for more and better translations of the Bible for the common people.

On April 18, 1521, Martin Luther stood before the Diet of the German nation to be tried as a heretic. In the face of excommunication and threatened death, Luther's words rang out firm and clear to the assembled throng of determined accusers and a few valiant friends: "My conscience is captive to the Word of God!" Unless convinced by Scripture or reasonable argument, he could not retract his teaching, he declared.

"These words of Martin Luther reflect both the compulsion and inspiration of the Reformation. The knowledge of the Bible was the motivating force which stirred the lives of millions, for whom the church had been the only mediator of divine salvation. The living Christ was unshackled from ecclesiastical bondage and the message of life became life and liberty for spiritually enslaved peoples." [1]

In the second place, the great revival movements of the eighteenth and nineteenth centuries found their primary inspiration in the rediscovery of the truths of the Bible. The revivals were nourished by study of the Scriptures. The Evangelical Awakening in Great Britain, for example, led by the Wesleys and Whitefield, followed the method of Pietism of organizing small groups for prayer and Bible study. In fact, the keynote of most of these "revivals" was the emphasis upon expository preaching—explaining and understanding the Word of God.

The third significant area for the use of the Scriptures in modern times has been the mission field, where consistently the Word of God in the languages of men has been the "cutting edge" of evangelism. The "great awakenings" in Britain and American inspired the "Great Century" of Protestant missions—the nineteenth century—and also produced the Bible and tract societies which were auxiliary to the mission boards. The Bible societies have had the major role in translat-

---

[1] Eugene A. Nida, *God's Word in Man's Language* (New York: Harper and Brothers, 1952), p. 82.

ing and distributing Scriptures in the "mission fields." In fact, correlations between the extent of Scripture distribution and the rate of church growth have been consistently high.

In the fourth place, "biblical renewal" has been a focal element in the dynamic changes which are now taking place in Roman Catholicism and in a number of important developments in Protestantism. Beneath the exciting movements involving revival of the laity, recovery of biblical evangelism, vital developments in theology, liturgical reform, expressions of Christian unity, and all the other aspects of church renewal, there is the influence of biblical truth. It is the rediscovery of the message of the Scriptures which has created the dynamic for spiritual renewal.

"The Word of God Is Living and Powerful"

J. B. Phillips, whose translation of the New Testament in modern English has conveyed its message with fresh power and relevance to many moderns, speaks of the "electric energy" of the New Testament.[2] One gets the impression from Dr. Phillips' testimony that the translator of the New Testament, like an electrician, discovered that he was working with materials charged with power.

"Although I did my utmost to preserve an emotional detachment," says Phillips, "I found again and again that the material under my hands was strangely alive; it spoke to my condition in the most uncanny way."[3] His vital encounter with the power of God's Word profoundly affected him. "I found myself provoked, challenged, stimulated, comforted, and generally convicted of my previous shallow knowledge of Holy Scripture," he declared. "The centuries seemed to melt away, and here I was confronted by eternal truths which my soul, however reluctantly, felt bound to accept."[4]

Thus in the written Word we encounter the living Word. The significance of the incarnation is that the divine Word (Jesus Christ) became life (human life); and the meaning of true faith is that the written Word may be translated into life, by those who understand it and are willing to live it. That is to say, the Word becomes life in the person of Jesus Christ, and then the written Word in turn becomes the medium through which the living Word confronts men

---

[2] J. B. Phillips. *Ring of Truth* (New York: The Macmillan Company. 1967) p. 73.
[3] *Ibid.*, p. 25.
[4] *Ibid.*, p. 24.

with the message of life. As the young man from Minneapolis said, "Whenever I read that book, someone seemed to keep speaking to me." Those who are willing to believe the message to the point of staking their lives upon it find life indeed. Only when a man has found something worth dying for has he discovered something worth living for. "For whoever would save his life will lose it, and whoever loses his life for my sake will find it" (Matt. 16:25, RSV).

Beyond the sacred page I seek Thee, Lord;
My spirit pants for Thee, O living Word.

2.
The Bible, a Book About You
Ralph A. Herring

The Bible is a book about you. Obviously such a sweeping statement needs qualification. It certainly is not a book exclusively about you. Nor, for that matter, is it a book exclusively about anyone else, not even God, who authored it. He determined its objective and planned the successive stages in the development of its theme. He gave to the mighty drama which the Bible unfolds its cosmic setting. He made the man Jesus Christ its unquestioned hero. But the nature of this man and of the conflict in which he engaged is precisely the reason for saying that the Bible is a book about you.

The remarkable thing about the Bible, then, is the fact that the better acquainted you become with its infinite scope and its variety of subject matter, the more clearly you understand yourself. The Bible is unique in this respect. It will tell you more about yourself than any other book you can read. At great pains the Author shows you who you are, what you are, what you may become, and how.

But this is not all. The revelation is not of you isolated from all others. Your heritage is exceedingly rich in depth and variety. It is interlocked on every level with others, and it is related to them both in time and eternity. Thus, what may seem an almost exclusively personal approach to the study of the Bible includes others, God most of all. If followed faithfully this approach brings one into the grand sweep of God's own point of view.

The artist considers with great care the perspective from which he wants his painting to be viewed. Though he works immediately by the canvas, he does so with the position of his viewer constantly in mind. Even so the reader is ever in the mind of the writer. The Bible is no exception to this principle. It can be best understood and its message most readily appropriate when those who study it appreciate their own important position in reference to all that was written.

A Bid for Interest

This natural and remarkably effective appeal for reader interest is the first great value. It engages attention at the point where it is most readily given. For example, if you are in a group picture, for whom do you look *first* when you see it on display? Or again, should a friend tell you about reading an article in the newspaper concerning what you did or said, how long would it be before you purchased a copy to read for yourself?

As the writer can testify, this same bid for interest holds true about the Book God has written. The first Bible I ever owned was given me by my mother when I was eight years old. How proud I was of its handsome leather binding! Opposite the title of the book of Genesis in a boyish scrawl there is an entry: "June 12th 1913 begin to read." Just when or where that high resolve played out I have often wondered. It did not last long. In the next decade, including a year at the seminary, my Bible reading was for the most part under compunction either of conscience for neglecting it so much or of necessity in the preparation of lessons at college and seminary.

It was in the fall of 1923, the year I taught school, that something happened which changed my whole attitude about Bible reading. I purchased a revised version of the New Testament of convenient size and readable print and began reading in Matthew. The daily portions were not long. Where one day's reading left off, the next day's reading began. I marked the passages that were of special interest to me.

Soon there came a surprising discovery. I found myself in the pages before me! They seemed to speak of my circumstances and problems; things that had perplexed me began to clear up. The book came alive. In the next six years ten dates were entered at Matthew, chapter one. Each marked a new reading of the New Testament, and the habit continues.

Tell a man that the Bible is a book about God, about heaven and the way to get there, or about hell and the way to avoid it, and he will thank you. He may even state his intention to read it sometime. But get him to see that it is a book about himself, about his present problems and predicaments, about the people whom he meets, and the chances are he will begin to read it.

This appeal is right and natural. It is the place where God began with man. After the tragedy of sin, God's first question to fallen man was, "Adam, where art thou?" It was not a question of one who sought information. God knew where Adam was. It was a question rather by which God sought to get with man right in the center of his own predicament. And that he still seeks to do.

Thus, there is a right sense in which every man stands in the center of his universe. An incident told of a young astronomy student illustrates the point. Overwhelmed by the immensity of space, he asked his teacher, "Astronomically speaking, what is man?" "Astronomically speaking," the teacher wisely replied, "man is the astronomer."

To this God agrees. He displays the panorama of nature to one in the midst of his own horizon. He stands with him under the center of his vaulted dome to direct his gaze heavenward just as he did with Abraham of old or with the author of Psalm 8. The message of the heavenly bodies is beamed individually today as it was to patriarch and psalmist. When God leads one through the pages of his Word, there can be no doubt that the warm rays of his light come to a focus directly upon the reader himself.

In such discovery there is nothing to exaggerate one's self-importance. Quite the contrary. The discovery leads to the profoundest humility. It creates the most "learnable" frame of mind a student can possess. This attitude is of special importance where the content is that of revealed truth.

A New Perspective

A new perspective often yields insights of priceless value, even when the object viewed is familiar. A challenging dimension in life opens up to the man who finds himself in the pages of God's Word. This is another advantage to consider in studying "The Bible, a Book About You." It yields a fresh appreciation not only of the content and arrangement of the Scriptures, but also of its overarching purpose.

Today if some man or group of men were trying to write a Bible, they would undoubtedly in some formal way authorize the doing of it. They would carefully note the date and circumstances under which each assigned portion was written. The name and qualifications of each writer, as well as the sources each used, would require strict documentation. But from the evidence in the Bible, God does not seem to have regarded such procedure as nearly so important as man does.

Again, man today would carefully edit his material, deleting every tedious and unnecessary passage, eliminating repetition, ironing out every inconsistency. This is an important contribution in any writing released to the public. God, too, must have had his editors, or the various writings would never have been brought together. But the way he let them go about their task seems careless and haphazard by today's exacting standards.

Another item in this conjectural contrast is the matter of organization. With his penchant for system, man would certainly organize his material on the basis of reason—chronologically or topically, with cross-references and indexes complete. The structure of the Bible shows God's distaste for artificiality, for the schemes and patterns so dear to man. Man's product would doubtless be informative and logical. But his book would never be called a living book, much less a life-giving book. And the Bible is precisely that.

If the organization of material in the Bible marks it as unique among other books, even more does the material or content itself. Of course, like any book, the Bible is made up of words, but what words! They flash pictures, vivid and powerful. Moving events come alive as God breaks through into the experiences of man. "He made known his ways unto Moses, his doings unto the children of Israel" (Psalm 103:7, ASV). These mighty acts range from creating the universe to supplying the daily needs of an obscure widow, from noting the sparrow's fall to recording the supreme tragedy of Calvary.

The telling of God's mighty acts marks the style of the Bible. Its profound insights are flashes struck from the anvil of experience. Drama was an essential element in the Temple ceremony. Doctrine was teaching in relation to conduct and character. Out of an encounter with the living God the Word came to poets and prophets. Even the law came to be regarded as testimony. It was a witness of God's righteousness in human experience. In the Bible God's mighty acts run the gamut of his redemptive activity. They involve nature and nations, human and cosmic destinies, time and eternity. Glimpses of such experiences set life in new dimensions. They provide the viewer a depth of field beyond anything like that obtainable elsewhere.

On the human level the choice and arrangement of materials in any book is a significant clue to its author's objective. What, then, does this unique structure of biblical content tell about God's purpose in the book that has come to be known as peculiarly his? Is it not precisely to provide the viewer with a depth of field beyond anything like that obtainable elsewhere, to set life for him in a new dimension? If so, a pattern of infinite care begins to emerge out of a putting together which once seemed carelessly left to chance.

One of the more recent achievements of photography has been the printing of pictures with an astonishing third dimensional effect. In such cases the camera operates as it travels on a track, describing an arc about the subject. Pictures are taken in rapid sequence and prints of each are made on transparencies incredibly thin. These are placed one upon another to form a composite picture. The result is a most realistic picture.

The Bible presents pictures of God's mighty acts in somewhat the same fashion. Their composite effect yields the startling reality of an entirely new dimension. For example, look at the tragic picture of Gehazi, Elisha's servant. There he stands stricken with leprosy in its advanced stage (2 Kings 5:27). This is the last in a series of word pictures. Look at the others: one, playing host in his heart to greed and covetousness; another, taking silver and raiment under false pretenses; yet another, lying to the man whom he knew to be the prophet of God. The composite effect is to reveal the spiritual background of Gehazi's physical malady.

The unique thing about this composite picture, and about other such pictures in the Bible, is the dimension of the spirit. For Gehazi's leprosy can never be really understood in terms of physical contagion alone. His case history, as God recorded it, included the unseen realm of the spirit. The disease of his body was revealed in relation to the disease of his soul. No X ray or test tube of man's invention could ever show this relation. But the Bible shows it. To become aware of this unseen background and of its bearing on all of life's situations is to realize the importance of the added dimension which can be seen only from God's perspective. There can be no complete understanding without it.

It has already been noted that the author of any book reveals his objective by his choice of an arrangement of materials. That being the case, it seems that God's objective in the Bible is to reveal himself preeminently but not exclusively. In finding God man is to find himself also, and this discovery adds an entirely new dimension to life.

The Word at Work

Once a man finds himself in the pages of the Bible another great value emerges with amazing effect. He begins then to tap the saving power that God transmits through the variety and vitality of its identity patterns. This flow of energy comes about because God identifies himself with the record of his mighty acts in such a matter that, as the reader identifies with them in the response of faith, the two of them—God and the reader—come to know each other in personal experience. This, of course, is the way anyone comes really to know another, not so much by information about him as by experiences with him. The point is that God is never far from his Word. Actually, he is in his Word and this is the secret of its power. As Paul wrote to the young church in Thessalonica: " . . . it is in truth, the word of God, which also *worketh in you* that believe" (1 Thess. 2:13, ASV).

How does the Bible *work?* The Scriptures themselves give a specific answer. "For the word of God is living, and active, and sharper than any two-edged sword, and piercing even to the dividing of soul and spirit, of both joints and marrow, and quick to discern the thoughts and intents of the heart" (Heb. 4:12, ASV).

The Word of God is alive and does work. Its function is described as searching, revealing, and judgmental. The phrase "quick to discern" is an effort to give the meaning of one word in the Greek. Transliterated it is *kritikos*—our word "critical, acting as judge." It highlights the judgmental quality of the Word. Thoughts and intents of the heart come under the searching light of God's truth. This is in keeping with what we have just been saying about the way in which the mighty acts of God are pictured. Here is an X-ray picture: "There is no creature that is not manifest in his sight: but all things are naked and laid open before the eyes of him with whom we have to do" (Heb. 4:13, ASV).

The phrase "with whom we have to do" is worthy of special note. The emphasis is on encounter. He who hears God becomes by that act responsibly involved in an encounter with him. He has business at hand to take up and complete. It is to avoid this very involvement that many turn a deaf ear to God and carefully bypass any serious study of his Word. They can't be bothered! Not understanding that God works through judgment to redemption, they make the uneasy decision to disregard both. But the Word continues to work—to some a savor from death unto death; to others a savor from life unto life.

These are some of the working principles which characterize the way of the Word. Consider now some examples from the Word which illustrate these principles in action. [1]

Biblical Examples of the Spoken Word

The first example will be that of Nathan the prophet, whom the Lord sent to reprove King David concerning his sin in taking Bathsheba, the wife of Uriah (2 Sam. 12:1-15). His message was in the form of a parable, or story. The shepherd king readily identified with the man who had been robbed of his sheep. Quickly he pronounced a just sentence upon the offender. Then came God's penetrating thrust: *"Thou* art the man." In the sudden light of an entirely new dimension, David saw himself as the guilty man and confessed. He said the same thing about himself that God had said, making his identification with God complete. And when he did that, God identified with David by putting away his sin.

Another revealing insight into the working of God's spoken Word is described in 1 Corinthians 14:23-25. The significance of this passage, however, is hardly apparent from the first reading. In order to get the picture it is necessary to have clearly in mind some facts in their larger context.

In chapter 14 Paul was writing to correct certain disorders in the Corinthian church which robbed their worship of its highest meaning. He was concerned particularly with the rule of the spoken Word in making worship a vital experience. This Word found expression in the gift of prophecy and in the gift of tongues. The spectacular nature of the latter gift made a special appeal to the Corinthian Christians, many of whom were making a display of it for prestigious purposes. Evaluating these two gifts upon the basis of edification, Paul came up rather bluntly with the conclusion: "In the church I had rather speak five words with my understanding, that I might instruct others also, than ten thousand words in a tongue" (v. 19, ASV).

Paul further confirmed his position by a quotation from Isaiah (vv. 20-22).

This brief resumé of the background is an introduction to the following verses selected for special study:

"If therefore the whole church be assembled together and all speak with tongues, and there come in men unlearned or unbelieving, will they not

---

[1] The distinction between both the spoken Word and the written Word is for convenience only. The same power operates both.

say that ye are mad? But if all prophesy, and there come in one unbelieving or unlearned, he is reproved by all, he is judged by all; the secrets of his heart are made manifest; and so he will fall down on his face and worship God, declaring that God is among you indeed" (1 Cor. 14:23-25, ASV).

Note that two situations are pictured here. Both of them are hypothetical, each being introduced by an "if." The first picture, although softened as an imagined case, bears an unmistakable resemblance to what was actually going on in the church at Corinth. Against the background of competition and confusion, Paul projects a second picture. It is the bright promise of what *could be* going on in Corinth *if* conditions were changed so as really to give the Word a chance.

In this latter scene the Word involves the very people whom every experience of corporate worship is intended to reach: the unbelieving and the uninformed. Observe that reactions to each are identical. The change from the plural (men) in verse 23 to the singular (one) in verse 24 is significant. However large the gathering, God's Word seeks men out one by one. Wherever it is given forth as it should be (v. 3) and received as it should be (v. 29), with discernment, the situation takes on an entirely new dimension. Eternity invades the present. In its searching light the unbelieving or unlearned discovers himself; and, vastly more—he discovers God.

The passage plainly shows that the function of God's Word is searching, revealing, and judgmental. From the nature of the case it must be so before it can become saving and sanctifying. Much is said about the critical approach to Bible study, and that is well. Bible students are under abiding debt of gratitude to critical scholarship, as will be seen in later chapters. But the real treasures of God's Word, its quickening insights and transforming power, are known only by those who bring themselves under the continuous judgment of its searching and cleansing light.[2]

---

[2] The situation pictured in the Corinthian church, of course, provides remarkable insight into the terrific power of what is called group dynamics. When persons meet in an atmosphere of mutual concern to face reality on a personal level, each forthrightly voicing the truth as he has been given to see it, the effect is searching indeed. By identifying first with one and then with another facet of the truth as others state it, the participant arrives at a composite picture of himself which is remarkably objective and often painfully candid. A confrontation of this kind is bound to develop pressures of fear and hostility. The question is: Will a man identify with the candid picture of himself which he has just seen? Or will he identify with the rosy picture he has entertained of himself and hopes he had projected among others? His problem is one of facing reality. If he makes his identification correctly and completely, the experience is therapeutic. Acceptance—his own and that of others—is its rewarding effect.

Biblical Examples of the Written Word

A great teacher once said, "Jesus dressed daily before the mirror of the Old Testament Scriptures." His figure of speech was scriptural. The Bible compares itself to a mirror. Paul says, "But we all, with unveiled face beholding as in a mirror the glory of the Lord, are transformed into the same image from glory to glory, even as from the Lord the Spirit" (2 Cor. 3:18, ASV). That the mirror refers to Scripture seems clear from the context.

An obvious application brought out by this comparison is that the service which a mirror renders lies in that which it reflects. One looks at it chiefly to see what otherwise is not in his line of vision. The devout reader of the Bible looks "beyond the sacred page" for a reflected image. There, according to Paul, he finds the Lord of glory. There, also, according to James, he sees himself as he is, "the face nature gave him" (Jas. 1:22-25, NEB). Between these two images the Spirit of God patiently works out a transformation from the natural to the supernatural, from glory to glory.

A show window in a large department store once featured a fur sale. Central in the display was a "magic" picture. Spectators were always before it. Cunningly imprinted on two different angles of one beaded surface were two contrasting scenes which alternated according to one's slightest shift in viewpoint. Now it was a beach scene in summertime; again it was a snow scene in midwinter!

God's Word reflects alternating pictures like that. It abounds in identity patterns which show the reader what he is and what he may become. This is what Christ, the Living Word, did for Simon. He showed him what he was (Simon) and what he would become (Cephas), Peter the Rock (John 1:42). This is what the Spirit did through Paul when he wrote about the role of the spoken Word in the worship experience at Corinth. He revealed the sad spectacle of what was going on in the church, but he also had a vision of what *might* be going on there. In the sense of being faultless, there were no ideal churches in New Testament days, but there is the *image* of an ideal church in the New Testament. Against the background of serious imperfections there appears a glorious reflection, a composite of what a church ought to be and can be by God's grace.

The candid picture of what man is may indeed cause shame but it will never cause despair. God does not show it without showing also the glory picture of what one may become. The two pictures are no case of trick photography, no gimmick to attract attention. The two scenes are real and the power of transformation from the picture of shame to the picture of glory is real too. Reading the Bible keeps a man face to face with two realities—the reality of sin and the reality of grace.

The hallmark of the Word of God is its power to change. This power inheres in the Word itself because God stands identified with what he says. Through his almighty Spirit he backs it up. He said to Jeremiah, "I watch over my word to perform it" (Jer. 1:12, ASV). Angels recognize this. Gabriel said to Mary concerning the miracle of the incarnation, "No word from God shall be void of power" (Luke 1:37, ASV). Repeatedly throughout the Bible, in direct statements and through many striking figures one is confronted with the power of the Word. The prophets knew no stronger guarantee of reality than that "the mouth of the Lord hath spoken it."

But this power is not mechanical. The function of the Word is personal. Its origin and its purpose are personal. Even in a mirror, where the reflection is necessarily mechanical, the power of transformation from one image to the other is personal. A man sees himself and straightens his tie. His response is personal and free. He believed what he saw and took appropriate action. The same man sees himself in the Word of God. He believes what he sees there, too. But his faith enlists the resources of Another far greater than himself. Because of that Other, the effect is saving and sanctifying—gloriously satisfying. The Book About You offers another tremendous advantage, the promise of fulfillment.

The Promise of Fulfillment

The bright promise of fulfillment is described in a verse of Scripture, a study of which concludes this chapter. The verse is in a highly emotional situation, Paul's leave-taking at Miletus. Concluding his exhortation to the elders of the church in Ephesus, among whom he had labored three years, he said: "And now I commend you to God and to his gracious word, which has power to build you up and give you your heritage among all who are dedicated to him" (Acts 20:32, NEB).

Note again the power of the Word. That power is described as a working force. It operates to bring God's heirs to maturity (see Gal. 4:1), making actually their own that heritage of glory which falls to each of them. The word "heritage" or "inheritance" deserves special attention. This great word reveals the nature and the degree of fulfillment which the Bible offers.

"Inheritance" is the translation of a word in the Greek (actually a compound of two words) meaning "the law of the lot." The picture in it accurately reflects what took place when Joshua led Israel to inherit the land of promise. The portion of each tribe in Israel was determined by casting lots before the Lord.

The figure implied by the word "inheritance" speaks with remarkable force today. The laws of heredity indicate that a man's lot in life is pretty well determined before his birth by a "chance" combination of genes. Yet he feels very deeply, although he may not be able to explain it, that the determination of his lot was "before the Lord." Intuitively he holds as God-given the inalienable right of a person to come into the dignity of his own selfhood. Paul's prayer was profoundly inclusive. As two drops of water sometimes coalesce to form one, the Word unites man's deepest need and God's highest fulfillment in one act of grace.

Another important thing in this prayer is its accent upon the role of the Word in bringing men to possess and to enjoy their inheritance. That role is logical and important. If one has indeed been born again, this miracle came about "not of corruptible seed, but of incorruptible, through the word of God, which liveth and abideth" (1 Pet. 1:23). The Word by which one becomes heir is the Word by which he also comes into his inheritance. The guarantee of doing so is the same as that given to Joshua. "Only be strong and very courageous, to observe to do according to all the law, . . . according to all that is written therein: for then thou shalt make thy way prosperous, and then thou shalt have good success" (Josh. 1:7-8). If one ever is to "come into his own" in the higher meaning of that fine phrase, it will be by the power of the Word.

This great prayer of Paul's seems to "wrap up" all that has been said concerning "The Bible, a Book About You." But the package is open-ended. The appeal in the chapter caption is valid. Is the Bible a book about you? Are your heritage and destiny *really* in it?

If your answers to these questions are in the affirmative, you are well launched upon a lifetime study. Your concern will be for the message of the Bible as a whole, not only for some favorite portion. You will acquire tools and develop skills for mining its riches and for sharing them with others. Above all, you will prize the company of the Living Word. But God will not let you stop with letters on a page. This world of people and life's swiftly changing situations all about you must become your laboratory where by the obedience of your faith you will release God's transforming power among men. The effect will be life-giving for them and for you. Together your progress will be from glory to glory.

3.

Understanding the Bible

Ralph A. Herring

Was ever in all literature a wordplay more effective than the pun with which Philip greeted the Ethiopian eunuch? "Well now," he asked the perplexed courtier, "do you really understand what you are reading?"

A pun, of course, defies translation. Suffice it to say that the force of Philip's wordplay was in the fact that certain particles of speech used with the Greek verb "to understand" made it sound like the verb "to read." With God-given insight Philip had probed the Ethiopian's real problem.

Astonishment showed upon his swarthy features. Astonishment occasioned not so much by the sudden interruption to his reading as by its timeliness. "How can I?" he answered. Then, hope breaking through his perplexity, he continued, "except someone shall guide me?"

Between Philip's pleasantry and the pathos of the eunuch's reply, one meets head-on man's great difficulty in understanding the Scriptures; namely, his penchant for matching the process of divine revelation with his own process of reasoning. Involved in the delicate interaction is the nature of revealed truth itself, man's capacity and his willingness to receive it, satanic interference, and the Holy Spirit's ministry to communication. For a better understanding of the Bible these varied elements ought to be recognized. Thus may one approach that body of truth which lies beyond the wisdom of man. To help him do so is the objective of the present chapter.

Revealed Truth

A first step in understanding the Scriptures is to realize that while much of it can be quite readily understood, its real wealth of meaning is a matter of spiritual insight rather than mental ability. The Bible draws a sharp distinction between truth known to man on the level of his own thinking and truth which is disclosed to him through an experience with God. The two terms commonly used to draw this distinction are reason and revelation. But in using these terms one must bear in mind that revelation has no quarrel with reason. Rather, the quarrel is with pride on the part of those who shut out all evidence that does not first qualify as reasonable to them. It is this pride which "rears its proud head against the knowledge of God" (2 Cor. 10:5, NEB).

Again, the use of the word "insight" must not be taken to mean that it distinguishes revealed truth from truth in the more general sense of the term, or that it denies the validity of insights which occur in the natural thought processes. The differentiation here is not in the manner in which a disclosure is made, but in the person who makes it. The Greek word for revelation is *apokalupsis* (apocalypse), an "unveiling," actually a "taking the cover off." The distinguishing mark of revealed truth is that it is God who takes the cover off, and not man. Note the delight of Jesus in response to Peter's great affirmation in Caesarea Philippi: "Blessed art thou, Simon Bar-Jonah: for flesh and blood hath not revealed *(apokalupsen)* it unto thee, but my Father who is in heaven" (Matt. 16:17, ASV).

There is another distinctive quality of revealed truth illustrated in this verse from Matthew. Its content is concerned with God as manifested in Christ Jesus. It is, therefore, essentially personal in nature, spiritual in dimension, and redemptive in purpose. Obviously, one may know much about a person by seeing him, hearing him talk, or observing what he does. This is true of God. Paul states that even the pagan has knowledge of God and is held responsible for it. "For the invisible things of him," he writes, "since the creation of the world are clearly seen, being perceived through the things that are made, even his everlasting power and divinity" (Rom. 1:20, ASV). But knowledge which is perceived in this manner is not enough. It is too external and objective to satisfy either the Creator or the creature who bears his image. In both God and man is the desire for that kind of knowing which comes only through experience. Without a direct and personal encounter one may know a great deal about God and yet not really know him.

To make that experience possible is the whole purpose of revealed truth. Throughout the Scriptures, in the law with its elaborate symbolism of tabernacle and temple, in the record of all kinds of events and their interpretations by prophets and apostles, and above all in the person of Jesus Christ his Son, God is making himself known in redemptive love. This is the grand motif of the Bible.

But there is this about love. Sometimes, but rarely, it expresses itself in bold declaration. It chooses rather, as every lover knows, the language of indirection. Love's strange logic is evident in those words from that disciple whom Jesus loved: "Now Jesus loved Martha, and her sister, and Lazarus. When therefore he heard that he was sick, he abode at that time two days in the place where he was" (John 11:5-6, ASV). What an illogical "therefore"! A lesser love would have rushed to the Bethany home. But God's love waits for the greater glory which only suffering can bring. It is important to know from the outset that as surely as God is love, the Bible is a love book. He has written it to man, love-starved, lonely, and lost. It is most readily understood when taken that way.

An Inherent Handicap

Another factor to be considered in understanding the Bible is the difficulty of the natural mind to receive its spiritual content. Before a man has been born again, there are dimensions of the Bible's truth which lie beyond his perception. In a classic passage to the Corinthians Paul clearly describes this difficulty. According to the New English Bible, he says: "A man who is unspiritual refuses what belongs to the Spirit of God; it is folly to him; he cannot grasp it, because it needs to be judged in the light of the Spirit" (1 Cor. 2:14, NEB). The word translated "unspiritual" here and in the Revised Standard Version is translated "natural" both in the King James and the American Standard versions. It is a key word, and to be understood it should be considered in the light of what Paul has just said about the "word of the cross."

The apostle in 1 Corinthians 1:18 to 2:16 is drawing a contrast between God's wisdom and that of this world. The conflict occurs at man's level of perception. God's wisdom requires a dimension of spirit which man in his natural state is incapable of grasping. Paul does not at this point explain what happened to block man's receptivity to truth on the plane of the spirit. But the inference is that this blight befell the human race when man first broke away from God through disobedience. The result of this tragedy is that although the words of the Scriptures are intelligible to man, yet without divine aid he lacks the power to relate them to the spiritual ideas which they express. Without experience in that realm he was no criterion of values. Consequently, truth, "the word of the cross" (1 Cor. 1:18, RSV), makes no sense to him. It simply does not add up; he rejects it as foolishness.

This is the tragedy of the world's wisdom as opposed to God's, of knowledge according to the flesh in contrast to that revealed through the Spirit. No man can reason his way through to God. Not even with all the paraphernalia of modern research can he do so. Paul wrote to the Corinthians, "the world through its wisdom knew not God" (1 Cor. 1:21, ASV). He was thinking of his visit to Athens, the most cultured city of all time, the home of philosophers, and the cradle of scientific thought. He found it full of idols. He found something else, too, and the memory of it haunted him. It was an altar bearing the inscription "To an Unknown God."

Communication of Revealed Truth

John records an incident in the life of Jesus which serves admirably as a transition from man's natural incapacity for revealed truth to God's breakthrough in communicating it. The story of Jesus and Nicodemus illustrates both the human problem and its divine solution.

In all the pages of the New Testament one hardly meets a more devout scholar than Nicodemus. Religious, upright in character, this cultured gentleman was a member of the Sanhedrin, esteemed as a teacher in Israel. Nicodemus began his interview with Jesus by courteously stating the conclusion to which he had come concerning Jesus. The inference is that he had verified the many signs wrought by this prophet from Nazareth. In the true scientific spirit he had assembled his data and from it had arrived by a clear process of logic to the fact that Jesus was a teacher come from God.

But somehow that conclusion did not satisfy him. Truth on the plane of reason never does. It was this inner dissatisfaction which brought Nicodemus that night to inquire further from the Master himself.

The answer of Jesus to the opening statement of his quest for a long time seemed to this writer to be painfully abrupt. I tried to justify it as our Lord's way of emphasizing the necessity of the new birth. But on the surface Christ's opening pronouncement seemed little related to what Nicodemus had just said. Then one day, as I read it in the original, something happened to remove this difficulty entirely. That something had to do with the word translated "see." I had taken it to mean that unless a man is born again he cannot even see the kingdom of God, let alone enter it. But the Greek for "see" is *idein*. Jesus was talking about getting the "idea" of the kingdom of God. That was what Nicodemus was searching for too, but he was going about it in the wrong way. Jesus made it plain that it could be found not through his powers of deduction but through an experience of grace so radical in nature that it could only be described as a birth from above.

It is important to understand that Jesus belittled neither the intelligence of Nicodemus nor his standing as a scholar. He simply highlighted, against the insufficiency of scholarship alone, the kind of truth which is revealed through an experience with God. There is no conflict between revealed truth and reason. Quite the contrary. Revealed truth presupposes and challenges the powers of intelligence. The conflict arises when pride of intellect forfeits the light available through revelation. It is not a case of reason or revelation but of both, plus the humility necessary to make the repentance-faith experiment. Take God's way to find God's truth.

God's method of communicating the saving truth of the gospel is by experience. To really understand the Bible, then, one must obey it—believe it to the extent of acting upon it, of committing oneself whole-weight to its truth for time and eternity. At a time when tremendous pressure was upon him, Simon Peter said, "Lord, to whom shall we go? Thou hast the words of eternal life. And we have believed and know [note the order] that thou are the Holy One of God" (John 6:68-69, ASV). As the writer of Hebrews has said, "By faith we understand" (11:3).

Satan's Opposition

A chapter devoted to hindrances and helps in understanding the Bible ought certainly to contain something about the opposition of Satan. All who take God's Word seriously will encounter resistance from this source. Satan will oppose them directly or by subtle use of agents and interpretation of circumstances. In this sophisticated age such a statement may seem crude, but facts are no less facts because they are spiritual in nature.

The Bible has a great deal to say about Satan. It takes him seriously. He is no minor character, no bugaboo or jester in this drama of redemption. He is the archenemy of God and man, with whom Jesus himself came to grips in a cosmic struggle and victory so great as to stagger the imagination of men. Next to Satan's enmity toward the Living Word is his opposition toward the written Word.

And no wonder! The Bible exposes him. It is the sole authoritative source of information about him. It gives broad hints of his origin and resources, describes his utter defeat by the One who is stronger than he, and discloses his ultimate destiny. To study the Bible is to become acquainted with his wiles. Therein the Christian warrior finds his equipment, the sword of the spirit, and other weapons mighty before God (Eph. 6:17; 2 Cor. 10:4).

The Serpent's strategy in regard to God's Word is quite evident in the temptation of Eve, as recorded in Genesis 3. There the tempter began with a question about what God had said. The battle is invariably drawn at this point. "Yea, hath God said?" (Gen. 3:1). What did he say? What did he really mean? Why? The deciever hurled the whole weight of his attack against the Word of God and man's obedience to it. This is the beachhead which he must secure first.

From this beginning the basic strategy of satanic opposition has been the same—ceaseless warfare against the message of the Bible. By every device of procrastination and diversion he opposes serious study of the Bible. He will smother, if possible, every intention to do so with a blanket of spiritual inertia. He takes advantage of man's suspicious nature to further his poisonous propaganda. Deceiver that he is, he works best in darkness and often provokes confusion to conceal his own identity. He makes much of pride, which, incidentally, seems to have been the occasion of his own downfall. He threatens and intimidates the believer with a show of strength entirely beyond that which he possesses. He capitalizes upon ignorance—of the Bible especially, misquoting it, setting one portion of it against another, impugning its authority, ridiculing it, twisting its meaning, crowding and confusing the reader into hopeless frustration. All these arts he has practiced with uncanny skill, one must be on guard against them.

Something of the bitterness of this conflict between Satan's lie and God's truth breaks through in a comment of Jesus as he gave the parable of the sower. The revealing phrase is marked in italics. "Then cometh the devil, and taketh away the word from their heart *that they might not believe and be saved"* (Luke 8:11, italics added). The purpose in all he does is unspeakably cruel. The same bitterness is evidenced in Paul's outburst of righteous indignation against Elymas the sorcerer, who was "doing his best to dissuade the proconsul [in Salamis] from accepting the Faith" (Acts 13:8, Phillips). Filled with the Holy Spirit, Paul looked him in the eye and said: "You son of the devil, you enemy of all true goodness, you monster of trickery and evil, is it not high time you gave up trying to pervert the truth of the Lord?" (Acts 13:10, Phillips).

These are strong words but they warn the student of Scripture that Satan's opposition to its revealed truth is relentless. One cannot naively bypass an adversary of this kind.

The Holy Spirit's Help

The transition now to a study of the Holy Spirit's help in understanding revealed truth is welcome indeed. Remember that the Holy Spirit is God. He is also Lord. He is the Spirit of truth and in that realm his sway is sovereign. He is, therefore, entirely capable of getting across to man what he wants said. And this he *will* do in one way or another, especially to those whose desire to know the truth is matched by their will to obey it.

In one sense the Holy Spirit is the author of the Bible—and more: He is compiler, editor and publisher, teacher and tutor, guide and administrator of its life-giving contents. He moves freely from one of these roles to another through the marvel of human instrumentality—without infringement upon personal integrity and without distortion of historical fact.

It may seem somewhat afield to speak of the Spirit in these terms. But does it not seem afield also to magnify the Holy Spirit's inspiration at the point of the original manuscripts and to overlook his sovereign grace working through history to make the Bible what it is today? The more involved the strategy, the greater the glory of the general who devises and executes it. By the same token, the complex process by which the Bible has come into being may evidence the Spirit's sovereignty on a level even higher than that of inspiring an individual writer. It involves more people, more servants of the Word, more varied talents, more tedious hours in the labor of love, more doctrinal battles waged and won, more dangers braved and victories gained. The triumph of truth is measured by the nature and extent of the opposition which it overcomes and by the effect it produces in the lives of those who obey it. Judged by these standards, the Bible is unique. Its glory surpasses that of all other books.

In communicating personal values, especially between loved ones, a letter is generally regarded as a poor substitute for conversation. But in the case of the Holy Spirit this advantage of personal contact is not limited to time and place as it is with men. He accompanies the written Word in person. It is he who first awakens an interest in its contents. The joy of his presence awaits only the recognition of the reader. Thus, the author of the Word becomes also its teacher and tutor. And more, he becomes the personal conductor and guide into its truth.

Two promises of Jesus describe this aspect of the Holy Spirit's ministry: In John 14:26, "the Comforter, which is the Holy Spirit, whom the Father will send in my name, he shall *teach* you all things." And again in John 16:13, "Howbeit when he, the Spirit of truth, is come, he will *guide* you into all the truth." The teacher becomes guide at the point where truth becomes experiential, and that is the significant thing for this study. Sin, repentance, the cross of Jesus, and the power of his resurrection are more than scriptural doctrines or theological concepts. They are *experiences* and no one can really understand them except as they become known through faith's experiment.

Considering the experiential nature of truth conveyed in Scripture, the role of the Holy Spirit as guide is most instructive. Any tourist can appreciate the force of the figure. He knows he must follow his guide, do as he says, look from his point of view, and above all, listen. And in an art gallery the sightseer will learn from his guide the importance of perspective and lighting. The Spirit's ministry is to illumine. "God . . . give you a spirit of wisdom and of revelation in the knowledge of him" is the prayer of Paul, who continues, "having the eyes of your hearts enlightened, that you may know . . ." (Eph. 1:17-18, RSV). In the light which the Spirit sheds upon the Scriptures the student makes a discovery for himself, and that is the important thing. It is the most dynamic element in the whole process of learning. Discovery makes a witness out of a man who otherwise would be only instructed.

One who has visited the Carlsbad Caverns will never forget two places far underground, the "Big Room" and the "Rock of Ages." At these points the guide stops to explain that for exactly a minute every light will be turned off to let his party know from experience what total darkness is like. To be plunged into Stygian blackness 780 feet beneath the surface of the earth has a sobering effect. The writer was reminded of the words of the Scriptures which describe the ninth plague in Egypt as "darkness that could be felt." It was assuring to hear the voice of the guide promising light in a moment. Then it came, flooding the vaulted cavern, cathedral-like, from hundreds of outlets. Colors sprang forth from the darkness in unimaginable and awesome beauty.

The Holy Spirit's ministry is like that. However intellectual and perceptive he may be, the natural man is in spiritual darkness. "Thought-benighted" he stands in the midst of a world of glorious reality which never becomes visible to him except by divine illumination. "The light of the gospel of the glory of Christ who is the image of God" may "dawn" upon him, or break like a sudden flash from heaven as it did in the case of Saul of Tarsus. How it comes depends upon the guide.

"When the spirit illumines the heart, then a part of man sees which never saw before; a part of him knows which never knew before, and that with a kind of knowing which the most acute thinker cannot imitate. He knows now in a deep and authoritative way, and what he knows needs no reasoned proof. His experience of knowing is above reason, immediate, perfectly convicting and inwardly satisfying." [1]

At the time when the New Testament was being written, there was a generally known and convenient analogy on the human level to the kind of truth which can be known only through the Spirit's illumination. Jesus himself and the writers of the New Testament, especially Paul, made free use of the word "mystery." There were many mystery cults which had sprung up as tribal religions broke down under the pressure of a world community. In New Testament usage a mystery was not something too difficult or profound for ordinary people to know. It was rather an open secret made known only to the initiated, to believers. These believers were in turn to make it known to others. Especially in the dark hour when faith is under trial, the Holy Spirit flashes some new insight from the Word to the eye of faith. In the floodlight of his illumination the believer comes to see the manifold wisdom of God's transcendent design as

---

[1] A. W. Tozer, *The Divine Conquest* (Christian Publication, Inc., 1950) p. 68.

revealed in Christ. Thus his progress is from glory to glory.

"The ministry of the Holy Spirit in relation to the believer and the Word of God may be summed up in three words: illumination, application, and appropriation. He supplies illumination by revealing its meaning to us. He makes application by convicting us of our condition in the light of its truth. He inspires appropriation by quickening its promises to challenge our faith. He did this for Jesus in his temptation (Matt. 4:4) and he will do it for us. This is the Word men live by—not the Word written and recorded long ago, but the Word which under the Spirit's quickening "proceedeth [note the tense] out of the mouth of God." [2]

The Learning Attitude

Much is being said today about the importance of continuing education. The stress is on continuing education as opposed to the old concept that at some point along the way, celebrated by academic pageantry, the student completes his education. All too many Christians have this concept about the things which God wants them to know.

But one who daily sits at the feet of the Master knows that today's emphasis on continuing education is not new. Jesus made much of it. "If you continue in my word," he said to those who had believed on him, "you are truly my disciples, and you will know the truth, and the truth will make you free" (John 8:31, RSV).[3] This idea of abiding in the truth in order to know the Truth which makes one really free challenges the motivation of every student of the Bible.

Mark tells how Jesus once interrupted his teaching to make an appeal for that attitude which would keep his disciples everlastingly learning from him (Mark 4:24-25). In this passage he first sounded a warning to us. The truth which he brings is judgmental, dynamic. Like electricity, it runs a circuit. What we get out of it will be measured on the scales which we ourselves provide. And more will be added. Then he stated what amounts to a law of learning: "He that hath, to him shall be given: and he that hath not, from him shall be taken even that which he hath." This law would be more readily understood if the translators had reflected the two meanings possible in the Greek

---

[2] Ralph A. Herring. *God Being My Helper* (Nashville: Broadman Press. 1955). p. 48.
[3] It is interesting to note how often the conclusion in this sentence is quoted by academicians with utter disregard to the condition upon which it rests.

word translated "hath" or "have." Actually, the Greeks had no word quite like the little and very important English word "get." Instead, they used a form of the verb "to have." The meaning is made plainer in a translation which observes this distinction. "He that gets, to him shall it be given, and he who gets not, even that which he has (at the start) will be taken from him."

In the kingdom of God the secret of successful learning is a continuing acquisitiveness on the part of the learner. Discipleship according to Jesus allows for no dropouts. There is to be no stopping. He wants his disciples (learners) diligently to get the meaning of his words, to see their application, to feel their challenge, to venture full-weight upon them in the response of faith, to traffic with them in the mart of eternal values. Thus may we keep learning of him in whom are hidden all the treasures of wisdom and knowledge.

4.

Interpreting the Bible

Frank Stagg

Professor W. O. Carver related to a class experience in which he as a young man sought help on a passage of Scripture.[1] He asked one of his teachers what a certain Scripture passage meant. The teacher answered, "It means what it says." The young student followed with a second question: "But what does it say?" All language requires interpretation. Language is an arrangement of symbols, spoken or written, through which one person seeks to communicate to another some idea, thought, feeling, intention, information, or something else. Meaning does not belong inherently to words, but words are vehicles which may help convey meaning; but this is true only because they are used that way. Man can associate meaning with words as he chooses.

That words do not inherently contain meaning may be demonstrated. What, for example, does "light" mean? It does not "mean" anything. It is an arbitrary symbol by which one may designate the opposite of darkness or the opposite of heaviness, or even the action of settling down, as when a bird "lights" upon a limb. Each language has its own word for a given object. This is conclusive evidence that there is no one-for-one relationship between a word and that to which it refers. A German says *Knabe*, a Greek says *pais*, a Frenchman says *garcon*, and an American says *boy*, and all may mean the same thing. On the other hand, when one says "boy," only context can indicate whether he is referring to a son or to a servant (cf. "my boy").

In the New Testament, as elsewhere, the same word is used to convey various meanings. For example, the Greek word *logos* is

---

[1] Dr. W. O. Carver was for about fifty years professor of missions in the Southern Baptist Theological Seminary.

translated in the King James Version as follows: word (218 times), saying (50), account (8), speech (8), Word (7), thing (7), matter (4), utterance (4), communication (3), reason (2), cause (1), talk (1), question (1), fame (1), rumor (1), treatise (1), tidings (1), interest (1), work (1), preaching (1), doctrine (1), and show (1).[2] On the other hand, the English word "left" translates nine different Greek words with such varying ideas as left hand, left over, abandoned, separation, etc. This is additional evidence that words have usage, not meaning. Of course, they come to us with certain associations and usages, but ultimately the speaker controls his words, they do not control him. Grammars and dictionaries indicate how words have been used, but only context can determine how a given writer uses a given form at a given time.

This is to say that communication is not easy. Language is filled with ambiguities. Every utterance has to be interpreted, and most utterances are capable of more than one interpretation. One might conclude that trying to understand another's intention is a guessing game. It is not that bad, for there are some well-tested principles which help one to understand another's effort at communication. No science of hermeneutics (interpretation) is foolproof, however. One must *want* to understand the other. But even when one listens or reads sympathetically, he may yet miss the other's meaning.

Distance adds to the problem of interpretation. This is true for the interpretation of the Bible. Almost two to three thousand years separate us from the biblical writers. They wrote in Hebrew or Aramaic (Old Testament) and in Greek (New Testament). Even translation from one language to another is interpretation. For an English-speaking American in the twentieth century, with all his conditioning as an American, to try to understand what was written two thousand years or more ago in some other language by a person of some other culture is a most difficult matter. But because the Bible is of utmost importance to us, it is indispensable to us that we try to bridge the gap so as to understand the intention of the Bible.

How Many Meanings?

It is now generally recognized that a passage of Scripture has only one meaning, although some passages may have intentionnally had

---

[2] Eugene Van Ness Goetchius. *The Language of the New Testament* (New York: Scribner's, 1965), pp. 18 f.

two meanings (cf. John 3:2, where Nicodemus may be thought of as being spiritually "in the dark" as well as having come to Jesus "by night"). For the most part, until the Reformation, interpreters sought multiple meanings in each passage of Scripture.[3]

Allegorical interpretation. For about a thousand years the allegorical method dominated Christian interpretation of the Bible. Origen (*ca.* 185-254) was a great scholar of Alexandria and Caesarea. He inherited much of the method of Philo, Jewish scholar of Alexandria (*ca.* 25 B.C.-A.D. 40). Philo had used the allegorical method in an effort to find Greek philosophy in the Old Testament. His object was to claim that Moses had already said what the Greek philosophers later said. To do this, Philo arbitrarily read into the Old Testament what he wanted to find there. Any word could be made to say what Philo wanted it to say. Origen and others after him followed this method.

Origen found three levels of meaning in the Scriptures: "flesh," "soul," and "spirit," although he usually developed only the first two meanings, the plain meaning and the deeper meaning. This method often led to ridiculous interpretations, as when Origen interpreted John 1:27 ("the lachet of whose shoe I am not worthy to unloose," ASV) to mean that few can solve the mystery of Christ's incarnation.[4] Origen's teacher, Clement of Alexandria (*ca.* 190-202), had followed the allegorical method. In the story of the prodigal son, for example, he found the robe to represent immorality, shoes to signify the upward progress of the soul, and the fatted calf to be Christ.[5] Such interpretation is not only absurd, it is disrespectful to the Bible and makes it a mere lackey to serve the interpreter's own ideas. This is "using" the Bible in the worst sense of "using."

It should be recognized that Paul made some use of allegory[6] (1 Cor. 5:6-8; 9:8-10; 10:1-11; and Gal. 4:21-31). He used the method only incidentally and occasionally. He built no major doctrine upon this method. Generally he employed the fulfillment principle, seeing the Old Testament to be fulfilled in the law.

Protest at Antioch. In Syria, chiefly in Antioch, serious attempt was made to interpret the Bible more honestly and completely. Some

[3] K. Grobel. "History and Principles of Interpretation." *The Interpreter's Dictionary of the Bible* (Nashville: Abingdon Press. 1962). II. 719.

[4] Cited by H. E. Dana and R. E. Glaze. *Interpreting the New Testament* (Nashville: Broadman Press. 1961). pp. 66 f.

[5] *Ibid.,* pp. 64 f.

[6] Cf. L. Mowry. "Allegory." *The Interpreter's Dictionary of the Bible.* I. 83.

of the great scholars who belonged to the "School of Antioch" were Diodorus of Tarsus (d. 394), Theodore of Mopsuestia (d. 428), Theodoret of Cyrrhus (d. 460), and Chrysostom (*ca.* 347-407).[7] These scholars sought to avoid the allegorical method and to stay closer to the literal meaning their effort was only partially successful, for although they rejected allegory they made much of typology; that is, they tended to find all New Testament ideas foreshadowed in the Old Testament. Typology easily fell victim to allegory, for in both the underlying assumption is that there is dual, if not plural, meaning in the Scriptures.[8] In fact, despite all the fine distinctions which ancient interpreters tried to make as they spoke of allegory, typology, tropology (moral), and anagoge (goal), these are basically the same type of interpretation.[9]

Triumph of allegory. The school of Antioch did not succeed in turning Christian scholars from the allegorical method. For about a thousand years interpreters in the Latin and Greek churches sought two, three, or four meanings in a text. The "spiritual" meaning was prized above the literal, and this spiritual meaning could be about anything to which the imagination was equal. A popular verse in Latin summed up a widely held theory of interpretation and may be rendered: "The letter teaches the events, allegory what you should believe, the moral sense what you should do, and anagoge that toward what you should strive."

Reformation recovery. Martin Luther and other reformers led the way toward a sounder principle of interpretation. Luther acknowledged the influence of Nicolas of Lyra, a Jewish scholar who helped break the tyranny of the allegorical method. Nicholas was a Franciscan professor in the University of Paris (d. *ca.* 1349) and was the author of the first commentary on the Bible to be printed (1471-72). He wrote eighty-five books, the first fifty of which sought the literal meaning, the remaining thirty-five the mystical meaning. Luther confesses that as a monk he was an expert in allegories and that he hated Nicolas of Lyra. Luther later repudiated the ascription of several meanings to a text, holding this to be a rejection of the authority of the Scriptures.[10]

Critical study today. The critical method today is used in most

[7] Grobel, *op. cit.*, p. 719.
[8] *Ibid.*, p. 720.
[9] E. C. Colwell. *The Study of the Bible* (Chicago: University of Chicago Press. 1937). p. 110.
[10] *Ibid.*, p. 723.

schools throughout the Christian world. It is used in various forms, varying degrees, and with different results; but most biblical scholars accept critical study as valid and proper. Even a great number of scholars who see themselves as theologically "conservative" employ what they call the "historical-critical" method of study. That is, they intend to study biblical writings in their historical settings, with some degree of objectivity, and through tested principles of interpretation. There is little resistance to textual criticism, except in the most isolated groups. Other levels of criticism are more often questioned, but when properly employed they are widely respected.

Principles for Interpretation

Martin Luther, in protest to the claims of the Roman Church that it alone was competent to interpret the Bible, declared that the Bible is *Allgemeinverstandlich*, that is, understandable to all men.[11] Luther's stand was a proper one, considering the background against which he made his protest. The Bible is intended for all people and all should have opportunity to read it. An open Bible and an open mind are important for all. No human institution has the right to deprive anyone of the privilege of or responsibility for reading the Bible and seeking out its meaning.

But the whole truth is not contained in Luther's claim that the Bible is "understandable to all." Interpretation is the scholar's task as well as every man's privilege. Much of the Bible is so plain and obvious as to meaning that it can be understood by any intelligent person without special training. At the same time, it is to be seen that much of the Bible is difficult, and its interpretation is more than a challenge to the most highly skilled scholar. Some passages in the Bible have baffled the ablest of biblical scholars. The task of interpretation, then, belongs to the untutored layman and the highly skilled specialist alike. It is important that layman and scholar labor together in the quest for a better understanding of the Scriptures.

In the chapter on the English Bible, it was seen that scholars like Wycliffe (Oxford) and Tyndale (Cambridge) risked or gave their lives in order that even the plowboy might be privileged to read the Scriptures in his own language. These scholars trusted the laymen and should have done so. It is proper for the layman to trust the

[11] This section on "Principles for Interpretation" somewhat parallels the author's *New Testament Theology* (Nashville: Broadman Press, 1962), pp. 10-12.

scholar and insist that he, too, have the right to interpret the Scriptures. Each is most secure in his study of the Bible, scholar and layman, when there is mutual trust and respect and when both engage in the study together. Within limits, the Bible is understandable to all; at points it requires the lifelong work of the specialist.

Critical and devotional. Bible study is best when it is both critical and devotional. Critical is not a negative term. As used here, it does not mean "to find fault." In popular usage that is what criticism means—finding fault. It is used here in a technical sense and in a positive sense. Critical study is a method by which one seeks answers on the basis of evidence. It means open, honest inquiry, a search for truth. Applied to biblical study, it means that one tries to be open to all evidences which would help him understand the nature and message of the Bible.

Devotional study is probably better understood than critical study; yet it, too, may be misunderstood. Devotion is misguided unless it is directed toward the real intention of the Scriptures. What is called devotional study may become devotion to oneself or to one's own thought. The allegorist, for example, merely reads his own thought and values into the Bible. If devotion is true to the Bible, it must also be "critical" in the best sense. True devotional study and true critical study have the same goal—to learn what the Bible itself has to say, not just what one may want it to say. Devotional and critical study go hand in hand as to purpose. Each wants to hear what God is saying through the Scriptures.

Objective and subjective. John A. Bengel in 1734 introduced his edition of the Greek New Testament with a Latin couplet, which in translation says: "Thy whole self apply to the text; the whole text apply to thyself." This combines the best of critical and devotional study. The interpreter is at his best when he brings to the study of the Bible his full self: intelligence, feeling, will, energy, plus all resources at his command—historical, grammatical, etc. He must also be willing to submit to the judgment and the instruction of the Scriptures, if he would learn their secrets.

This is to say that the study of the Bible is to be objective and subjective. It is to be objective in the sense that one begins with questions and evidence, not with answers. He does not force the Bible to support his views, but he tries to be open to the biblical truth, whatever it may do to positions, beliefs, and values already held.

But biblical study is not like observing a chemical test in a test tube. It is personal. It is the effort of a person to understand the persons who wrote. One is not studying just literature; he is studying Mark, Paul, or John. Beyond that, he is a person seeking to hear God, best known as personal. To this extent biblical study is subjective as well as objective. It is to be sufficiently objective to safeguard one against bias, prejudice, or dogmatism. It is to be sufficiently subjective to mean personal involvement. The Bible best yields its treasures to the one who comes to it with all the skills available to him but who also comes to it with submissiveness and devotion.

Wholeness. The Bible is best studied as a whole. The poorest interpretation is by the "proof text" method, building upon isolated verses. Context is not only important for interpretation, it is indispensable. It is only in context that words and grammatical construction acquire meaning. Any statement of a writer is best interpreted in the light of all that he has written.

No doctrine should be built upon a passage in which the subject is incidental. For example, Paul says something about those "baptized for the dead" in 1 Corinthians 15:29. The subject is introduced in a long passage about the resurrection. The chapter is a primary one for understanding Paul's doctrine of resurrection, for that is his subject. Though the Corinthians undoubtedly were familiar with the occasion for this reference, Paul does not say enough on this subject to make his meaning clear to his readers now. It is a safe principle, therefore, not to use this (or any other) obscure passage as a proof text since it conflicts with other passages clearly set forth elsewhere. Paul risked his life to proclaim that circumcision cannot save a person. It is inconceivable that he would turn right around and say that water baptism can do what flesh circumcision cannot, that one could be baptized for another! It is only fair to Paul to assume that in 1 Corinthians 15:29 he does not contradict his whole Christian life.

Individual and community. Bible study is proper for any individual, but it is also a community endeavor. In a sense one may work alone but he is wrong if he thinks that he can really work alone. At every point he is dependent upon words coined by other people and upon information and insights gained from the labors of others. Peter warned that "no prophecy of scripture is of private interpretation" (2 Peter 1:20, ASV). God does not grant private disclosures that are withheld from other people. This does not mean that some do not see or hear more clearly than others. Great voices like those of Moses, Amos, John the Baptist, and Paul ring out and lead others to new dimensions in the understanding of God. But even these men were not "loners," isolated from others. They, too, built upon foundations laid by others and learned from the community of which they were a part.

This principle is strikingly set forth in Ephesians 3:18, where the prayer is that the readers be able to grasp "with all the saints" the great love of Christ. It is when we find ourselves in the fellowship of God's people that we are in the best position to understand his Word. This means that we should enter into meaningful dialogue with all God's people of our time and with his people across the ages. This may be done in part by wide reading of what others have written in our time and in times past. The only thing worse than the provincialism, which limits one's exposure to his immediate group, is the isolation of the "loner" who tries to go it alone. We can learn much even from those with whom we must often differ. Various Christian groups have contributed to the learning and literature by which we all benefit. For example, the King James Version of the Bible was the work of the Church of England; Cruden's Concordance came to us from the Presbyterian tradition in Scotland; and our great commentaries come from men of various churches. Our hymnals include hymns from many Christian groups. No individual or group has a monopoly upon the truth or upon the understanding of the Bible. We can best study it "with all the saints."

Perspective. It is important to understand the perspective of any writer. Although biblical interpretation means that one is studying actual writings, it is the writer behind the writing whom one wants to understand. As far as possible, each writer is to be known and understood in terms of his own personality and conditioning. It is true that one is to be understood in terms of what he does and says, but it is also true that what one does and says is to be interpreted in the light of the person himself. To illustrate, when one meets a stranger, one can form only tentative judgments of him by what he does and says. But after having come to know another, one tends to understand what he does and says in terms of the person himself. When an adverse report on a trusted friend is received, one is disposed to say, "I do not know why he did or said that, but I know my friend, and I believe that when more is known about his action he will be vindicated." Thus, Paul may be understood from the things he wrote; however, what he wrote may also be understood from what is known of the man himself.

A case in point would be things Paul wrote about baptism. Did he believe that water baptism saves (cf. Gal. 3:27 f.; Rom. 6:3-11; 1 Cor. 12:12 f.)? When one sees that he risked everything in consistently taking the position that circumcision does not save (cf. Rom. 2:25-29; Gal. 5:6), and when one sees that he distinguished between "circumcision, in the flesh, made by hands" and "circumcision not made with hands" (Eph. 2:11; Col. 2:11, ASV), he can be sure that Paul did not mean that water baptism saves. No sane or consistent man could reject flesh circumcision yet affirm water baptism as saving. This is to say, it is not enough simply to interpret writings. It is important to try to understand the man behind the writings.

Although each biblical writer has his own individuality and his own perspective, there are also some perspectives common to biblical writers in general. For example, all New Testament writers are in some way testifying to Jesus Christ. The New Testament is *Christuszeugnis*, witness to Christ. Through the New Testament, the Old Testament is also seen to be witness to Christ (Luke 24:27; John 5:39). Eschatology is a view of history. It is faith's understanding of history as being under the control of God and, under God, as being carried forward to its goal *(eschaton)*. The whole Bible is eschatological not just Daniel, Mark 13, Revelation, and passages here and there. On the negative side, this goal is judgment; on the positive side, it is redemption. Both redemption and judgment are already in process, but both await their completion at the end or goal of history. The whole Bible is written from this perspective.

Things to Consider

Critical study of biblical literature includes at least six questions: Who? When? Where? To whom? Why? What? These questions represent an inquiry into authorship, date, place of composition, audience, purpose, and content.[12] These are questions examined in books known as "introductions" or "introductions to the literature of the Bible." Any writing is more understandable if the life situation behind the writing is known. It is helpful to know the author, who he was, and what factors shaped his thought and life. It is helpful to know the

---

[12] Colwell, *op. cit.*, p. 126.

first readers, their background, problems, needs, and interests. If the immediate occasion for the writing is known, that gives one a great advantage in understanding the writing.

For example, it helps to know that the Thessalonian letters were written by Paul to young Christians who were troubled by disappointments, fears, and misunderstandings with respect to the return of the Lord. It helps one to understand the Corinthian letters to know the highly complex relationship between Paul and the Corinthians, including exchanges of visits and letters, misunderstanding of Christian freedom, and other specific problems. The study of Romans can be greatly enhanced by attention to the momentous decision which Paul had just made to turn back from Rome and Spain in favor of a trip to Jerusalem, taking an offering designed to bring Jewish and Gentile Christians into a better relationship with one another *(koinonia)*. The understanding of the Epistle of James is made more difficult because we know so little about the life situation out of which it came.

A writing should be seen in its wholeness; it is not enough to study isolated sentences. It is well to seek out the main purpose as well as secondary purposes or interests in a given writing. If a writer has employed sources, it is instructive to see how he used his sources. His own special interests are seen both in the sources selected and in how he employed them.

The structure or outline of a writing is important to critical study. One should be cautioned against imposing one's own neat outline upon a biblical writing. It does not necessarily follow that a biblical writer first made a careful outline and then followed it. Writers sometimes digress. Sometimes they deal with varied subject matter and various interests or problems without great concern for literary unity and sequence. It is proper to try to trace the author's own course of thought, but it is misleading to impose upon another's writing one's own sense of order.

Levels of Criticism

Critical study has traditonally been divided into "lower" and "higher" criticism. These terms are arbitrary and easily misunderstood. Lower criticism refers to textual criticism. Higher criticism refers to the many investigations of the writing after its text has been established.

Textual or lower criticism is the effort to recover the original text of a writing. All biblical writings were first written by hand (manuscript). They were preserved and multiplied through many centuries by manuscript copies. Each copying was subject to error. To err is human, and no scribe has ever copied a book without making changes, deliberate and unintentional. There are thousands of biblical manuscripts made before printing was invented (fifteenth century), and in these manuscripts are thousands of variants. Some scholars have to devote much of their lives to the difficult science of textual criticism. Every interpreter, without exception, either investigates the text for himself or accepts the work of textual critics. Each printed Bible, whether in Hebrew, Greek, English, or some other language, represents someone's work in textual criticism.

Higher criticism includes various special studies: form criticism, source criticism, redaction criticism, and all the concerns of literary criticism referred to under "Things to Consider." Form criticism is the effort to get back to the earliest units of tradition as formed and transmitted orally (see chap. 5). Source criticism is concerned with identifying oral and written sources which a writer may have used. Redaction criticism is the effort to see the writer's own hand in his employment of sources, his theological and other interests. Of course, much of this is highly specialized and is beyond the competence of all except the specialists. It does not follow that one has to be a specialist in all these levels of criticism in order to study the Bible seriously. Any literate person may enter into serious study of the Bible. It is to be recognized, however, that all of these areas of investigation are important. It means that biblical study is a team effort. No scholar can do everything, and certainly the layman cannot do everything. Each must depend upon the work of others. If one works from a Hebrew or Greek Bible, he works with a text already established by textual critics. If one works from an English Bible, he begins by accepting the work of textual critics and linguists who have translated Hebrew and Greek into English. If he uses a commentary or even a dictionary, he draws upon the labors of others. This is inescapable, and it is as it should be.

Application to Life

Two questions which properly belong together are: What *did* a biblical writing mean? What *does* it mean? First, one should try to learn what the writer intended to say to his first readers in terms of their situation. Only then may one turn to the question of what the writing has to say to us today. Both questions are important. The first without the second would be merely academic or of antiquarian interest. The second without the first would be the mere use of a biblical writing as a peg upon which to hang our thoughts. The Bible is relevant; one does not have to make it relevant. It is proper to see *what* its relevance is. This is done by trying first to see the writing in its own life situation and then to hear its lasting message for our situation.

One example may help. The problem of "meats sacrificed to idols" (1 Cor. 8:1-13) no longer concerns us as such. In today's supermarkets one does not find meat which has been offered as a sacrifice in pagan temples. But all of the issues which arose in connection with this problem at Corinth still exist. However, as Paul dealt with a local problem in his day, he set forth some lasting principles. Here are some of them, without which we cannot live in community with others. Christian freedom is never to be enjoyed with indifference to its effects on a brother. The other's conscience is to be respected even if wrong. It is not right to ignore the other's conscience, and it is not enough to embolden a "weaker brother" to ignore his own conscience. Neither is it sufficient for the "strong" simply to give in to the weak. The conscience of the other is to be respected, but one also has the responsibility to enlighten it. Christians are neither to be indifferent to one another nor to run over one another. They are to engage together in a shared life, both respecting and seeking to enlighten the other's conscience.

Library Helps to Biblical Study

Every serious student of the Bible should, as far as his resources permit, build his own working library. If he does not read Hebrew and Greek, he should secure one or more dependable translations. The American Standard Version (1901) and its revision as the *New American Standard Bible* (1963) are both highly serviceable. Most of the translations during the twentieth century are competent, although no translation is perfect or final. A good concordance is indispensable. The best ones in English today are Robert Young's *Analytical Concordance to the Bible* (22nd Am. ed. rev.; Grand Rapids: Wm. B. Eerdman's, 1955); James Strong's *Exhaustive Concordance of the Bible* (26th printing; Nashville: Abingdon Press, 1965); and Nelson's *Complete Concordance of the Revised Standard Version of the Bible* (New York: Thomas Nelson and Sons, 1957). A valuable source of information is *The Interpreter's Dictionary of the Bible* (Nashville: Abingdon Press, 1962). The four volumes of this dictionary contain articles by scholars from all over the world. They represent different faiths and points of view. Consequently, no reader will agree with all that he finds in these volumes, yet they are rich in information and insight, covering every major subject in the Bible. Possibly the best single-volume commentary is *Peake's Bible Commentary* (New York: Thomas Nelson and Sons, 1962). These books will refer to various commentaries and other scholarly works. They give bibliographies on almost any subject of interest to the Bible student. Frederick W. Danker's *Multipurpose Tools for Bible Study* (St. Louis: Concordia Publishing House, 1960) is helpful in introducing the student to sources and tools for Bible study.

5.
Unity in Diversity
J. Wesley Ingles

The Bible, as we have noted, is a literary anthology. Every nation has produced such a collection of literary materials by different authors and from different periods, but the Bible is unique. Unlike such collections from other nations, this anthology has a single developing and unifying theme. Some works by a single author, such as Homer's *Iliad* or Cervantes' *Don Quixote*, may have an underlying structure which draws together many dissimilar parts into an organic whole. But there is no collection of writings in the world that has such a striking unity as the Bible or so vast, so majestic, and so significant a theme.

To appreciate the miracle of the underlying unity in the apparent diversity of the Hebrew and Christian Scriptures, one should compare it with a historical anthology of the literature of the British people covering writings produced from its earliest times to the present. It would begin with the first extant epic, *Beowulf,* written in Old English. The only manuscript of this work dates from about A.D. 1000, but the poem itself is believed to go back to the first half of the eighth century, and some of the events to which it refers may go back to the early sixth century. By a strange coincidence, such an anthology of British literature would cover about as many centuries as the Bible does, more than a thousand years. But what a difference one would note in the two collections!

An anthology of British literature not only ranges from the adventurous Anglo-Saxon epic of *Beowulf* to the subtle contemporary poetry and plays of T. S. Eliot, but it includes all sorts of contradictory and conflicting points of view. The Christian perspective would be dominant through many of the centuries but the work of atheists, deists, humanists, utilitarians, positivists, perverts, and individualistic rebels of all types would be included in any representative anthology. There is no coherent, unified perspective discernible in the collection. It is a potpourri of everything of literary distinction regardless of point of view. It does obviously reflect the development of British culture, its life and thought through the centuries. But through it there runs no great and central theme. There is no discoverable *telos*, no unique and overarching purpose, drawing it all together.

However, when we study the biblical collection of writings, we discover that it is an organically related whole, bound together in a living structure. Like all that has life, it grows, changes, develops, but always in relation to the characteristics implanted in the original embryonic material. Within, underneath, and running throughout the biblical collection, we can observe a single developing and unifying theme.

This central and controlling theme of the Bible is God's purpose for man revealed in human history. It is seen first in a Chosen People through whom the nations of the earth were to be blessed. Then, at a focal point in history, it is seen again in a Person by whose life and death men would be directed into the way everlasting and eventually delivered from the follies and failures of their own sin. The theme is a revelation of the redemptive acts of God in history, guiding and directing its stream to the divine event toward which the whole creation moves, the establishment of a Kingdom of redeemed men that will have no end.

God's Redemptive Purpose Through a Nation

The Adamic race. In the Adamic race, whenever and wherever it began, the Bible declares that God was making a creature who would reflect something of his own nature and who would be able to respond to his Spirit. But the story of our race is a record of repeated failure, of a falling away from God and his purpose for man.

The Old Testament books recount the stages in which the Adamic fall was symbolically re-enacted: first, in the murder of Abel by his brother Cain, and then in the Sethite line through whom the initial purpose was to be carried forward. But this race also fell away until only Noah and his family were saved from the general destruction of God's judgment.

But degeneration and evil set in again, along with man's pride in his own achievements. Men would build a sky-reaching tower. The

city of man had no need of God, they thought. How often has this
illusion been vainly attempted in human history! How the false dream
of the secular city of man has corrupted our twentieth-century hope
for a world of peace and order! As T. S. Eliot wrote in the choruses
for "The Rock":

> We build in vain unless the Lord build with us.
> Can you keep the city that the Lord keeps not with you?
> A thousand policemen directing the traffic
> Cannot tell you why you come or where you go.
> A colony of cavies or a horde of active marmots
> Build better than they that build without the Lord.
> Where there is no temple there shall be no homes,
> Though you have shelters and institutions . . .

And so Genesis gives us a symbolic account of the confusion of
tongues around the tower of human pride at Babel. But how many
readers see the relation between this symbolic event and the miracle
of Pentecost recounted in Acts? Where communication was con-
founded by human pride, it was recovered by an outpouring of the
Spirit of God on men, inspired and renewed and commissioned as
agents of reconciliation. Here is another example of the amazing unity
of the biblical books. The New Testament Scriptures constantly play
back upon and illuminate the Old Testament writings.

The patriarchs. However, out of the corruption of the Babylonian
degeneracy, God once more calls out a people. From Ur of the
Chaldees, Abraham begins his long trek, at first with his father Terah
and then on his own with his wife Sarah, to a land of promise.

And after a tragic lapse of faith that brought Ishmael, child of
the bondwoman, into the world, there was finally the child of promise,
Isaac. Jesus in the Gospels, Paul in various epistles, and the author
of Hebrews all relate subordinate themes to God's great act in the
calling of Abraham and in the creating of Israel through his descend-
ants, Isaac and Jacob. The great theme, God's purpose for man, is
growing, developing slowly, revealing itself in history and especially
in the history of a people.

Bondage and Exodus. We can trace the long preparation of this
people in Egypt amid a great culture which in spite of its glory and
grandeur was far removed from the true and living God. Here in
an alien culture the tribe is to be shaped into a people. The redemptive
mission of Joseph is one of the great epic narratives of the Bible,

full of striking parallels to the life and mission of our Lord.

The sons of Israel succeed too well in Egypt. The Egyptians grow jealous and decide to reduce them to slavery or to destroy them. But once again God raises up a deliverer. Moses is trained in the house of Pharaoh and called to lead God's people out of the land of their bondage to be God's witness to the nations as he had chosen them to be.

Instead of being the vehicle of his purpose, even on the way to the land promised to Abraham and to his seed, they fail and falter and deny God in the wilderness. They lose faith in his purpose for them. But in the midst of their faithlessness, God gives them his law and his ordinances. And he gives them the symbolic pattern of a tabernacle in the wilderness that was to foreshadow the great Temple in Jerusalem and ultimately the spiritual temple built upon our Lord, the cornerstone.

The law given through Moses is to become the moral foundation not only of the Hebrew theocracy, but of all later civilizations affected by it through the spread of Christianity. And in the spiritual law given on the Mount by the Incarnate Lord and recorded in the Gospels, the law given to Moses is not superseded but transcended. In Christ the Mosaic law is not destroyed but fulfilled. And ultimately, in his redeeming death and triumphant resurrection there is established a new relationship between sinful man and God. The new life in Christ is no longer based on a legalistic effort to keep perfectly the law. It is based on a realization of pardon and acceptance through the perfect sacrifice of God's Son and the obligation of thankful love to live out God's creative and forgiving love in every human relationship.

Nevertheless, the giving of the law through Moses was the high point of the sojourn of God's people out of the land of bondage. They became the carriers of the moral ideal.

The conquest. The faithless perish in the wilderness, never reaching the Promised Land. But after the death of Moses, some of the people, a faithful and heroic remnant, push on under the leadership of his successor, Joshua, into the land which the Lord had given them. The whole story of Joshua and the conquest of Canaan is full of drama and interest.

Having conquered the land, the children of Israel begin to build homes and cities, to plant olive groves and vineyards, to herd sheep and raise cattle, and indeed to build a kingdom. Beginning under Saul, their first king, they rise to a new national strength under David, and reach the pinnacle of their worldly glory under Solomon. The borders of their land are extended, the holy city of Jerusalem bears the wonder of Solomon's Temple, traffic and commerce spread throughout the Mediterranean world, and the reputation of the little nation extends with it. Alliances are made and emissaries come from many lands to see the rising star of Israel.

The united kingdom. But Solomon, like Saul, begins well and ends badly. He takes wives and concubines, even from pagan peoples. He is rich and powerful and reputed to be wise. But the spirit of humility in which he began his reign disappears. He is now one of the great kings of the earth, and his people prosper and flourish at first, but from king to commoner they have forgotten their mission. They have forgotten that they were called out to be God-revealers, to make him known among the sons of men, to bring the light of his truth into the pagan world.

The divided kingdom. Following the death of Solomon, there is a struggle for power. There is treachery, division, hatred, and civil strife. The tribes, once united, are rent like a worn-out garment. The people sink into idolatry and immorality. The witness they were called to bear is fouled and polluted and desecrated. They have become like the nations about them and are eventually delivered into captivity and exile in Babylon.

But God is never without a witness. He raised up prophet after prophet to speak his word, men who without fear denounced the corrupt leaders and challenged the selfish people, and risked their own lives to proclaim the unpleasant truth as they had received it.

The prophets. This section of the Scriptures, known as the major and minor prophets, is one of the most amazing collections of writings in the whole history of literature. Here, in powerful and sometimes bitter prose, but more generally in passages of exalted and burning poetry, the prophets seek to arouse the conscience of their people. They try to call them to repentance and lead them back to the purpose for which God had delivered them from Egypt. But the people continually revert to the worship of other gods, lifeless deities who do not condemn their immorality, and especially to the worship of the symbolic golden calf and the luxuries it represents for the few while many struggle in poverty and lose almost all sense of their human dignity. Corruption and extortion and sexual promiscuity prevail.

The messages of the prophets were generally delivered orally, and thus when written, they preserve the poetic rhythms of the orator and the startling images of the seer.

It is important to remember that the term "prophet" given to this strange and wonderful group of men in Israel's history does not refer primarily to the predictive *foretelling* of future events as we have come to think of it, but to the oracular *forth-telling* of a truth from a mystical source. They were consciously spokesmen for God, bearing upon themselves sometimes unwillingly, the heavy burden of the word of God. As it was primarily the duty of the priest to speak to God for men, interceding on behalf of men, so it was primarily the duty of the prophet to speak to men on behalf of God, often to speak with lips touched with fire from the altar.

And these strange men, these great poets and seers, were generally amazing combinations of the mystical and the practical, of the idealistic and the realistic. They saw visions and dreamed dreams, they sometimes looked into the unknown future with extrasensory perception, but more often they looked about them with even keener insight. They saw with penetrating vision the cruel injustices in the society of their time, and they spoke out regardless of the cost to themselves. They knew that the inexorable mills of cause and effect would slowly and surely grind down those who would go on heedless of the divine purpose and the moral order God had ordained for man. From the time of Moses to Malachi the prophetic office passed from man to man by the mysterious and unpredictable calling of the Spirit of God. Holy men spoke as they were moved by the Spirit.

There is no more rewarding and challenging study in the Old Testament than these books of the prophets from Isaiah to Malachi. These were men proclaiming God's purpose in the midst of crisis and confusion, amid war and pestilence, in the revolutionary events of their times. They speak with a peculiar relevance to our time also, for they had a philosophy of history. They looked beyond the desolations and destruction, beyond the exile and dispersion of their unhappy people, to a day of glorious restoration when the kingdoms of this world would be overthrown like the colossal statue which Nebuchadnezzar saw in his dream and which Daniel interpreted for him as a symbolic image of human government in historical forms. He saw a stone not cut by human hands smash the image and begin to grow until it became a mountain filling the earth, a Kingdom of justice and righteousness and peace that would have no end.

God's Redemptive Purpose Through a Person

In the prophecies of Isaiah, we can see a transition to the second aspect of the Bible's basic theme. In this book we have most fully developed the revelation of God's redemptive purpose for man, not only in a people chosen to embody and reveal that purpose, but supremely in a Person, the Messiah, the Anointed One, the Redeemer-King, the Suffering Servant of Isaiah 53. And it is toward his coming and the establishment of his peaceable Kingdom that the visions recorded in Isaiah look forward. In this second aspect of the central theme, we can see most clearly the organic unity of the whole Bible, Old and New Testaments, the way in which the New illumines and completes the Old.

The title "Messiah" had become attached to the idea of a descendant of the Davidic line who would become a great deliverer of his people and who would establish a triumphant earthly kingdom superior to David's and Solomon's. Around this concept had gathered all the hopes of the Jewish people. The writers of the New Testament books were men who had come to see that all this, and much more that remained obscure, was fulfilled in the person of Jesus the Messiah. And the church was seen as the new Israel to be made up of those from all nations and tribes and races who recognize and acknowledge Jesus as the long-awaited Messiah of Israel and as the Lord and Savior of all men.

It was not only the references to the Messiah in the prophets, however, that convinced the early followers of Jesus. They began to see that their Hebrew Scriptures were all bound together in the concept of the Suffering Servant. From their earliest sacrifices, they had been taught the idea of vicarious atonement, a life given for lives. Abraham was taught this long before the night of the Passover escape from Egypt, long before the plan of the tabernacle set the altar of sacrifice at the center of their worship. And in the grandest designs of their later temples, Solomon's and Herod's, it was still there. A lamb slain, perpetually prefiguring the Lamb of God who alone could take away the sin of the world, was the central symbol in their worship.

But the Jews had failed to see this concept related to their promised Messiah. By the time Jesus was born, most Jews were expecting a king and conqueror who would enable them to throw off the hated Roman yoke and lead them again to glory among the nations. They did not understand that the Son of man must suffer to enter into his glory. Their minds were as darkened in their understanding of their own Scriptures as was that of the Gentile eunuch from Ethiopia to whom Philip was directed on the road to Gaza. Philip discovered that the Ethiopian was reading the fifty-third chapter of Isaiah as he journeyed home from Jerusalem. He was mystified by the Scriptures' awful portrait of the Suffering Servant. And beginning with that great passage Philip told to him the good news of Jesus.

In the Gospels. What the law and the prophets prefigured by many intricate designs in one purposeful pattern, the Gospels described as history. The different emphases of each Gospel when put together give a three-dimensional portrait of the Servant-King. In his life and ministry, in his death and resurrection, all the varied elements and poetic symbols are gathered together into a satisfying fulfillment—and that with a timing utterly inexplicable apart from the divine purpose.

All four Gospels concentrate on the closing days of this absolutely unique Life, and on the account of his triumph over death. The Passover meal is given new meaning. The paschal lamb is no longer needed because the Lamb has been slain once for all. The elements of bread and wine are now used to symbolize perpetually his finished sacrifice. The veil of the Temple is rent so that now the holy of holies is open. The throne of grace is directly accessible to the humblest believer through him who was both sacrifice and High Priest.

Although the rulers of the Jews and their misled people failed to see the fulfillment of their hopes, there were those whose eyes were opened to the spiritual nature of the Kingdom. Those who received Jesus as Lord were empowered by an outpouring of the Spirit to go forth into all the world to proclaim the good news of man's deliverance. They lifted up before all men the one ordained from the foundation of the world to redeem and restore God's lost creation. Thousands heard their message and believed and were added to the church, the new Israel.

At first the followers of Jesus did not fully recognize the worldwide nature of their commission. They did not at first fully recover the mission committed to Abraham and to his seed. They did not fully see that in them might shine the glory of the one true God and through them *all* nations of the earth might be blessed.

In the Letters. But again God had his witness, his prophet. He raised up one who would recover the mission of Israel to the world. Like Jeremiah, Saul of Tarsus came to believe that before he was formed in the womb God had called him to be a proclaimer of Christ, the Messiah, to the Gentiles. And so he not only traveled throughout the Roman world establishing little colonies of the Faith, but with his keen mind, trained in the learning of both Greeks and Hebrews, he brought together in his epistles a great intellectual and spiritual synthesis of all that the Old Testament had prefigured concerning the Son of God.

Here in the letters of Paul is set forth the theology that has shaped and stimulated the thought of the church throughout the Christian era. For centuries, some of his most tremendous spiritual insights were lost or corrupted. But when Paul's insights in his letters, to the Romans and to the Galatians particularly, were recovered by men like Luther and Zwingli, Calvin and Knox, they set some branches of the church singing again with joy in their spiritual freedom and with love for their divine Redeemer.

The letters of Paul to churches and to individuals, along with the general epistles by other writers, are absolutely necessary to a full understanding of Jesus the Messiah-King as presented in the Gospels. Indeed some of these letters were written before some of the Gospels. They present a record of ideas and practices already current in the young churches spread thinly across the Roman Empire. They explain the mighty acts of God associated with the incarnation of the divine nature in his Son.

In these letters, we discover that the new creation, the new society made up of new men and women, has begun to take root and grow. Little colonies of heaven are established in various places, and people made new in Christ begin to live out the new life, and astonish (and sometimes anger!) the pagan world with the quality of that life. The world may continue on its tragic course away from God and toward its own destruction, but the communities of the redeemed and committed are to be agents of reconciliation, ambassadors for God, reconciling lost and alienated men first to God and then to one another.

This is the continuing plan and the only hope for our fallen race which the Bible sets forth. History moves toward a consummation in time and a transcending of time.

Conclusion

And so the Bible comes full circle. It began with the symbolic fall of man from God's purpose and design for him. Forced from the garden of innocence by that fall, disobedient Adam and Eve are pictured pathetically wending their solitary way from Eden with its tree of life.

As the Bible began with poetic symbols, so it ends. There is another tree of life, bearing twelve kinds of fruit, set beside a river of life. And the leaves of the tree are for the healing of the nations. And for the redeemed servants of God there is no more sorrow or weeping, no more sickness or pain, and no more death. And there is no night in this eternal city, for the Lord God is their light forever.

Between the tree of Genesis and the tree of Revelation the Bible records man's long and tragic pilgrimage toward the light: stumbling, falling, sinning, rising, dreaming, hoping, longing for final deliverance. And set in the midst of the story—between the two trees—is another tree, a dead tree bearing a dead body of a Suffering Servant who would not stay dead because he was Lord of Life. And in spite of everything that might seem to argue against the full expansion of his Kingdom into all the earth, it will surely and finally come in its fullness because his word is sure and has already been supported by the strange fulfillment of its predictions in history.

This is the theme that draws the Bible together into its amazing unity as the Book of books. Written over so many centuries by so many different authors in so many different styles, the unifying theme of this anthology makes the Bible a single work, unique in the world's literature.

6.
The Bible Communicates Through Prose

J. Wesley Ingles

The Bible is the most amazing collection of writings in the world's literature, not only because of its enormous and enduring influence on the lives of men and nations, but also because of the variety of the types of writing and the extent of the times represented within it. Although developed over many centuries in diverse forms and styles, the whole collection manifests a strange underlying unity of purpose and of themes.

There are various approaches to the study of this complex work. Among them are the historical, the theological, the devotional, and the homiletical. Several of these approaches are used in different sections of this book. These are all necessary because they supplement and assist one another. But there is yet another approach to Bible study too often neglected: the consideration of the literary forms and styles in which the revelation was communicated.

To a proper study of the Bible we need to bring not only reverent scholarship, not only spiritual understanding, but also an imaginative response to its literary power and beauty.

Some may ask why an imaginative response to literary power and beauty is necessary to a full appreciation of the biblical message. The answer is in the form of another question. Why did God choose to communicate his revelation to man in literary forms and styles, some of them among the most artistic and aesthetically beautiful in all literature? Why did the revelation not come in the form of a textbook such as this, directly addressed to the reader's intelligence and understanding alone?

Obviously, just as the Incarnate Word, God's Son, came in human form and in human terms to appeal to the whole of our nature, so the written Word was embodied (incarnated) in such literary forms as would appeal to the imagination, would address the intelligence and the emotions simultaneously, and would convey truth in concrete rather than in abstract terms.

What is the relation of form to content, of method to message? Do the style and structure of a sermon have any significant relation to the ideas to be shared, the effects to be achieved? Can a careless stringing together of words and sentences or a coldly logical analysis have the same effect upon hearers as a sermon clearly constructed, warmly felt, and strongly delivered? Logically, message and method may be distinguished from each other, but actually they are integrally related in the effects they produce. The reader cannot fully appreciate one without regarding the other any more than he can appreciate a human personality divorced from its manifestations in and through the body.

The same is true of the service of worship. A slovenly, irreverent, careless procedure, as informal and sometimes as noisy as a political gathering, may entertain the thoughtless person but can only make the thoughtful grieve. God ordered solemn forms for his worship which invoked reverent awe. Form and content are both important. Beauty is an aid to worship. We can see the evidence of God's concern for this in the natural world, his picture book, as well as in the written revelation.

Therefore, to appreciate the literary art of the biblical writings, we need to analyze the beauty and structure, the style and form of its various types. For this great work is not merely a collection of quotable quotes or proof texts to settle theological arguments. If we read it thus, we do not begin to feel its power.

The Bible contains examples of almost all of the literary forms: the epic, the short story, history, biography, drama, poetry, proverbs, letters, and fantasy. Unfortunately, most Bibles do not reveal these significant differences in the format of their pages. It is almost impossible to enter into this kind of appreciation if we confine our reading to the double-column, separate-verse format. We need to use an edition such as Richard Moulton's *The Modern Reader's Bible* [1] or the more recent *Jerusalem Bible*,[2] if we are to "see" and hence to "feel" the structural forms, the linear parallelisms, and the rhythmical cadences that enrich our understanding and deepen our response to

---

[1] Richard Moulton. *The Modern Reader's Bible* (London: Macmillan Co., 1912).

[2] Alexander Jones. ed.. *Jerusalem Bible* (New York: Doubleday. 1967).

the great passages of the Bible.

In this chapter we shall look first at the prose types in biblical literature since most people seem to have less difficulty with prose than with poetry. Actually, in some works they are intertwined and cannot always be clearly distinguished. Poetry, as we shall see in the next chapter, lays greater stress on rhythm and imagery than does prose, and it is essentially figurative rather than literal. In order to interpret and appreciate these two basic types of writing, it is important to understand what each is intended to do and by what means it seeks to communicate to the reader or hearer.

The Epic

The Bible opens with an epic, one of the great ancient literary forms. The classical epic was a narrative of heroic acting, usually recording the exploits of a national or racial hero.

Genesis begins with a cosmic epic of creation, the origin of all things. In this majestic, profound account, so different in its grand utterance from the almost ludicrous myths of the pagan polytheistic religions, the language is suited to the high theme. The heavens and the earth, the stars and the planets are whirled into being and fixed in their courses by the will and word of an omnipotent Creator. The earth is clad in verdure; forms of life are spawned in the sea, on the land, and in the air. Man is shaped and breathed into sentient life to become a unique being in his relationship with his Creator. He is capable of fellowship with God, of growth toward him; but he is also capable of disobedience to the divine will and purpose.

As we read the biblical account of the origin of things, we become aware of a beautiful parallelism, a literary cadence of great power and beauty. Each creative day begins with the poetic repetition of the divine fiat: "And God said . . . And God said, 'Let there be . . . Let there be . . .,' " followed by the grand, simple assertion "And it was so . . . And it was so." Each day concludes with the recurring divine assertion of satisfaction in his creative work, "And God saw that it was good . . . And God saw that it was good."

Only as the reader's eyes see and his ears begin to hear these mighty reverberations can he begin to experience the rolling grandeur of the biblical epic of creation. And unless he rises imaginatively to this daring effort of the writer's mind to suggest the dawn of our solar system, our heaven and earth, he remains a smaller man, his mind unstretched by the supremely mysterious event. Even the most brilliant contemporary astrophysicist, with the help of all his scientific symbols, could not so powerfully describe the mystery as does the author of the Genesis story.

The subsequent account of the creation of man and of his fall is given in terms less grand, but no less dignified. The beauty and pathos of this frail but intelligent creature's growing awareness of his world, of himself, and of his need of a mate are told in a narrative that is both simple and profound. The birth of conscience, the violation of the inner law, the sense of shame, the bickering attempt to shift the blame, are narrated within the brief limits of a short story but with every sentence so full of valid psychological implications that the most learned English poet, Milton, was moved to develop it into the greatest epic in English literature, *Paradise Lost*. But Milton's immense work, placing the drama in its cosmic setting, is only an imaginative extension of and poetic embroidery upon the marvelously compressed and suggestive account in Genesis.

This is true of the other latent epics in the Old Testament. They are never developed as were the narratives in the classical Greek and Roman epics. But the epic grandeur is there, nevertheless. The accounts have been the inspiration for many later works of the imagination by writers trying to fill out the stories implicit in the biblical narratives.

Another cosmic epic is suggested in the awesome story of the tremendous destruction of the flood. This, and accounts of later cataclysmic events, are reported not only in biblical literature but in the literatures of all ancient peoples. This strange fact made such an impression on one of the most comprehensive and original thinkers of our time, Immanuel Velikovsky, that he has published a series of books based on the records of these events as found in literature and in scientific evidence pertaining to our earth.[3] The biblical account is told in powerful prose, rising and falling like the flood and ebb of mighty waters.

The classical epics of the world's literature are concerned chiefly with the heroic, with stories that have gathered about national or racial heroes. Epics of this sort are found in the Bible also, but, as indicated earlier, they are not fully developed, although powerfully

---

[3] Among his books are *Worlds in Collision, Earth in Upheaval*, and *Ages in Chaos*.

suggested. In fact, there is an unforgettable series of these accounts of great men, the heroes of faith.

These true and inspiring narratives undoubtedly developed out of folklore, narrated orally and passed from generation to generation. It was the most primitive form of narrative. Folklore may be based on real incidents, as here, but it is orally narrated. By the time the tales were incorporated in the Pentateuch, they had achieved a dignity of style which, although more literary than their spoken form, were nevertheless rooted in an earthy realism. This type of realism was characteristic of the Elizabethan period of English literature, which came just prior to the translation of the Bible by scholars appointed by King James. Indeed, such earthy realism was similar to that of our own times.

Consider first the story of Abraham, father of the faithful and founder of the tribe that was to become the Chosen People through whom God's written revelation and his Incarnate Son were to come. Following the strange call of this man out of Ur, we see him subjected to testing after testing. After repeated lapses, we see his final triumph of faith in the offering of his son Isaac, the child of faith. The dramatic power with which the epic narrative rises to this awful moment of crisis is one of the great achievements of narrative art.

To gain the full effect of this climactic moment, one needs to read at one time the whole story of Abraham and Sarah to see it moving by the rugged steps of dramatic ascent and fall to the ultimate triumph of faith in God's divine purpose. In the light of the New Testament revelation we can see the beautifully symbolic pattern in the action. But there is an ironic reversal because God the Father did not withhold his Son from the brutal sacrifice from which Isaac was saved by the vicarious death of the ram provided by God.

From the epic of the founding of the Hebrew people as a family, one moves on to another—that of their journey into Egypt. There the family was saved through Joseph, chosen by God to be the suffering and the saving servant of his people. In this epic we see the establishment of the tribe that would become twelve tribes. Eventually a people would emerge that would affect the course of history, that would stand ultimately uncrushed to the end of time in spite of every effort to scatter and destroy it.

The story of Joseph illustrates the amazing combination of epic dignity of style with the earthy and concrete realism of detail that makes great literature graphic and moving. But how many readers of the Bible stories visualize the action, share emotionally the experiences described? How many feel the basic and universal human emotions conveyed in the narrative?

One's interest is gripped by the series of dramatic contrasts in the life of Joseph, the repeated alternation of success and failure, of hope and defeat. But his discouragement never becomes despair, for this man trusts God completely. After the attempted seduction by Potiphar's wife, so frankly suggested, and the final deliverance from prison, we see Joseph rise to the highest position in the land, just under Pharaoh. Then famine brings his guilty brothers to Egypt, to the one whom they had betrayed. Seldom, if ever, has the plot of concealed identity been used with greater power nor has a character in fiction ever used his superior knowledge more dramatically than did Joseph in his final self-revelation.

In order to feel the emotional power in this story, one needs to notice the significant details, the realistic human touches which are the lifeblood of great writing. When Joseph first sees his younger brother Benjamin, his mother's son, he rushes out of the public room to a private chamber where he can give release to the great emotion sweeping over him. He weeps uncontrollably. There is no more moving sight than that of a strong man weeping. Just here is a revealing detail that makes the whole experience real: he washed his face, undoubtedly to reduce the redness in his eyes and to conceal his overpowering emotion. Afterward he comes out to his brothers and they eat—he, the great ruler, seated by himself, surveying the table of those who had betrayed him.

The deceptive trick of the cup which Joseph played on the brother fills them with fear. But this is the dramatic preparation for the big scene. Joseph sends all of the Egyptians away and there in the great hall makes himself known to his brothers. But again he cannot control his emotion and weeps aloud so that the Egyptians hear it. When he can finally control his voice, he says, "I am Joseph. Is my father still alive?"

Until a reader has heard that statement and that question after the storm of a man weeping, he has not felt the power inherent in great literature. The sound of it should reverberate not only in the house of Pharaoh but in the home, in the study, and in the classroom—wherever it is read. This is to re-experience the past, to feel the presentness of the past. And this is what the great narratives of the Bible can do for us—if we read them as literature and not merely as lessons for Sunday School or as text material for a sermon.

Probably the greatest biblical epic of all is the story of the deliverance of the Hebrews from Egypt under the leadership of Moses, the giving of the Law and the long wanderings in the wilderness before the conquest of the Promised Land under Joshua. Grand, full of energy and power, alive with drama and action, this is the high plateau of Old Testament narrative in its mighty span.

Short Stories

Old Testament stories. Yet, it is not only in the great epic tales that one is impressed by the skill in narration, but it is in the short stories as well. Sometimes the realistic details of these narratives, embedded everywhere in Hebrew history, are shocking. They are as brutal or horrifying as anything in Faulkner's novels. There is the episode of Noah, drunk and indecently uncovered before his son. There is the corruption in Sodom, horribly but dramatically depicted. There is the Greek-like story of Judah's incestuous relations with his daughter-in-law, Tamar, with its dramatic devices of the gifts by which she proves that Judah is responsible for her pregnancy. And there is probably the most shocking story of all—the origin of the war between the tribe of Benjamin and the other tribes of Israel with the violated body of a woman divided into twelve pieces, one sent to each of the tribes of Israel.

There is violence and brutality in the biblical narratives. These episodes are described not in general but in concrete terms. They are told so graphically that they register unforgettably on the mind. A number of these most graphic scenes are found in the book of the Judges, the record of a primitive stage in the history of Israel. We read that the people of Israel repeatedly "did what was evil in the sight of the Lord, forgetting the Lord their God." And repeatedly the Lord strengthened their enemies against them. But when the people of Israel realized their sin and cried to the Lord, he raised up for them a deliverer, again and again.

There is the story of Ehud, a Benjaminite, in which we are given the interesting detail that he was left-handed. Ehud is sent as emissary from Israel to convey the tribute they were forced to pay to Eglon, the king of Moab. Just here the details bring the brief story startlingly to life. Ehud makes a short two-edged sword, a cubit in length, the length of a man's forearm, or about eighteen inches. As he enters the king's presence with men bearing the tribute, he conceals the sword "on his right thigh" under his clothes. We are told that the king was very fat. After presenting the tribute, Ehud sent away his men, approached the king and says, "I have a secret message for you, O King." At this the king dismisses his attendants, whereupon Ehud draws the short sword with his left hand and thrusts it into the king's belly. The narrator gives the gruesome picture of a sword-thrust so violent that it was driven up to the hilt, the hilt itself being buried in the man's fat.

Judged by Christian standards, this assassination is horrifying. Equally shocking and equally graphic is the episode that follows, recounting the way in which Jael lures the fleeing Sisera, commander of the Canaanite army, into her tent. Pretending to conceal him from his pursuers, she gives him milk to drink, persuades him to lie down, and covers him with a rug. When he has fallen asleep in weariness, she takes a tent peg and a hammer and drives the peg into the side of his head with such violence that it goes through to the ground.

As one reads these bloody tales, he is forced to feel afresh and powerfully the evil and horror of war, the folly and tragedy of human enmity. But we feel these emotions because the events are so graphically narrated.

Fortunately, it is not alone tales of violence that have this almost incredible power to recreate a scene in words. There are also tales of love and beauty, of devotion and simple faith. The most famous of these probably is the pastoral idyl of Ruth. As a short story, this is one of the best in the world's literature. Set in the days of the Judges, the unsettled and troubled times of so much violence, the story tells of a man, his wife, and their two sons who went down to Moab to escape a famine in Judah. They decided to stay. The father died and the two sons married Moabite women. But the sons also died and the Hebrew woman, Naomi, decided to return to her native land. Her daughters-in-law accompanied her on the way, but at the border of her land she pled with them to return to their own people. One of them went back, but Ruth clung to her mother-in-law and pledged her faithful devotion in words that are perhaps the most beautiful expression of loyalty in literature. "Entreat me not to leave you or to return from following you; for where you go I will go, and where you lodge I will lodge; your people shall be my people, and your God my God" (Ruth 1:16, RSV).

And so they went together to Bethlehem. The existential decision was made and it led the widow Ruth to an adventure, to a love, and to a second marriage that placed her in the ancestral line of the Messiah. Her son would be the grandfather of David. A momentous choice indeed she made, not knowing to what it would lead her. But she ventured in faith, as did all the biblical heroes.

It is the quiet simplicity with which this pastoral tale is told that makes it so beautifully effective. The quaint ritual of the threshing floor by which Ruth persuaded Boaz to accept the responsibility of kinsman to perpetuate Naomi's line was reproduced in speech and action which conveyed perfectly the mood. As still and as lovely as a Flemish painting is the scene. And this tale of a night in Bethlehem prepares us strangely for another night in that town and for another Child.

The story of Esther is far removed from the pastoral scene. Here we are in a great foreign court at Susa, the capital of Persia. In the palace the fate of the captive Hebrew people hangs upon the beauty and courage of a young woman, Esther, an orphan brought up by her cousin Mordecai.

We sometimes forget that Ahasuerus, the tyrannical ruler of the story, was the Xerxes of Greek history. It was he who launched a great invasion against Greece. The invasion failed and the Persians were turned back at Salamis.

The palace at Susa, the banquet hall, and the revelry there are described in vivid detail. The steps by which Esther, the lovely Jewish girl, becomes the king's wife in place of Vashti and the awful responsibility for her people which comes to rest upon her are narrated in that kind of detail that lifts history into art.

The envy and hatred of Haman are revealed; his dark plot to destroy Mordecai and massacre all the Jews is unfolded with all the horrible fascination of Iago's plot to destroy Othello in Shakespeare's great play. The tension mounts and the burden on Esther to become the savior of her people becomes almost unbearable. She tries to escape the responsibility, but Mordecai will not permit that. His words, like those of Ruth to Naomi, are now among the most famous ever spoken. He sent a messenger to Esther to say:

Think not that in the king's palace you will escape anymore than all the other Jews. For if you keep silence at such a time as this, relief and deliverance will rise for the Jews from another quarter, but you and your father's house will perish. And who knows whether you have not come to the kingdom for such a time as this? (Esther 4:13-14, RSV).

Here it is worth noting how sharp and realistic is the dialogue in these stories. Unfortunately again, to save space, the stories in the average Bible are printed in a format which does not exhibit the dramatic nature of the dialogue, for it is run together in paragraphs of narration. In fiction today each speech by a different speaker forms a new paragraph; thus, the dialogue stands out on the page. If we were to print (or copy) the dramatic passages of the Bible in that manner, we would be surprised to see how much dialogue there is and how dramatically effective it is.

After Esther called her people to fast and pray, she sent word that she would intercede for them. "If I perish, I perish," she declared. The story mounts to its climax, a moment of fearful suspense when the fate of the Jewish people in Persia rests on Esther's acceptance by the king. The story then descends on the other side of that crisis to the irony of Haman, who is hung on the gallows which he had prepared for Mordecai. That is what the Greeks called "poetic justice."

Time would fail us to list the literary skills with which other biblical tales are narrated. Suffice it to say that beside the gripping content of the stories themselves, one can trace the hand of the literary artist in their telling.

Especially well told are the stories of Elijah and his successor Elisha; of Naaman the leper and the little Israelite girl who introduced him to the prophet, who brought about his healing; and of Jonah. The last is told with such dramatic force and power that one is swept along with Jonah into the incredible sea adventure of that God-fugitive.

In the story of Jonah, and in others, one easily identifies with the characters. For instance, reading with empathy the account of the return from exile, one is with Ezra as he rebuilds the Temple, and with Nehemiah as he rebuilds the walls. We stand with the crowd on the first day of the seventh month in the square before the Water Gate. We hear Ezra read from the book of the law of Moses. Standing on a wooden pulpit, he reads from early morning until midday. When he blesses the Lord, the great God, all the people answer, "Amen, Amen." They bow their heads and worship the Lord with their faces to the ground. And if we are wise, we do the same.

New Testament stories. But not all the moving and graphic stories are in the Old Testament. The Gospels demonstrate that Jesus was a master storyteller. He was the world's greatest Teacher. One of the chief reasons for the unforgettable clarity and force in his teaching method was his repeated use of concrete illustrations. He left nothing hanging in vague abstractions, such as would confuse and bewilder the uninitiated.

One of his favorite literary devices was the parable. This literary form is a short narrative, generally no longer than a vignette, which conveys a moral truth or spiritual insight by means of a carefully selected analogy. It embodies an abstract idea in concrete, living form. The parable differs from the allegory, which is a prolonged narrative metaphor in which all the parts and personages are representative of something else. Each element in a parable should not be required to yield some symbolic truth. Normally the parable contains one basic idea in its central symbol and the other elements should not be pressed for meaning. This, mistakenly, has been done sometimes by over-imaginative interpreters and has led to some confusing if not absurd interpretations.

The parables, like the other stories in the Bible, are beautifully exact in concrete details. But unlike the historical or folk tales, they are told primarily to illustrate and embody some great truth. Jesus apparently used this device not only to make real an abstraction, but to force the hearer to think, to reflect on what he was saying. The hearer was required to interpret the symbolic meaning.

Publicly Jesus would not assist in the interpretation, but privately he did so to his disciples. On one occasion at least we have the record. Great crowds had gathered about him as he sat by the Sea of Galilee. The press was so heavy that he had to get into a boat and talk across a little stretch of water. He talked about a field and a sower, about seeds and the various kinds of soil upon which the seed was sown, and about the varied results. Afterward, when his disciples questioned him about the meaning, Jesus seemed disturbed by their obtuseness but he gave the interpretation. Mark's account of this episode and others like it tells us that in private "he explained everything to his own disciples."

A few of the parables are recorded in all three of the Synoptic Gospels. Fewer still are recorded in only two Gospels, the majority of them appearing in either Matthew's or Luke's account. But the most famous of the parables occur in Luke's Gospel. Luke seems to have been the writer who researched and retold the narratives in their most beautiful form.

In Luke we read the shocking and disturbing story of a rich, selfish man and a beggar, Lazarus. Also in Luke is the moving and disquieting story of "the good Samaritan." Too often some modern readers fail to get "the point" of this terribly penetrating story by which every Christian today must be judged and must judge himself. Too often it is thought of as basically a story about a kindly man who helped a brother man in need when others had neglected him. But Jesus deliberately contrasted a despised and segregated Samaritan with people of his own race, the Jews, who had failed in charity. To understand the sort of courage it required to tell this story, one would need to think of a German pastor in the time of Hitler telling the story of "the good Jew," or of a white minister in our own time telling the story of "the good Negro."

The most beautiful of the parables and the richest in multiple meanings is also retold by Luke. It is generally referred to as the story of "the prodigal son," but it could with almost equal appropriateness be called "the forgiving father," or "the unforgiving brother," for these are all important themes in the story. Even critics who are not Christian consider this the most perfect "short short" story ever told or written. They are impressed by the almost incredible economy of means by which the effects are achieved. In our version it is well under five hundred words in length. Yet, the characters are dramatically presented and individualized, the three themes are balanced and inter-related, and the setting and situation are concretely and graphically sketched. Here is storytelling at its unforgettable best, a narrative of moving and universal human interest. Nevertheless, it contains ideas of the most compelling and enduring significance for our relations with God and with one another.

Of course, the narratives about Jesus in the Gospels are told with a similar skill. The miracles, the compassionate experiences, the conflicts, the turbulent crises are conveyed in language both terse and dramatic. All four Gospels mount with a swift intensity to the awful events of the closing days of our Lord's earthly life and mission. When placed beside the cosmic drama of that final week—the trial, the crucifixion, the resurrection—the greatest plays of Shakespeare sink to a lower level, as do most other plays, by comparison. This is truly "the greatest story ever told," and the writers of the Gospels were granted words suited to convey the earthshaking message.

When we move into the narrative of the subsequent events in the book of the Acts, we are again fascinated by Luke's skills as a writer. The defeated, broken, confused disciples emerge from the horrifying catastrophe of their Lord's death with new power and courage, the best and really incontrovertible evidence of the resurrection. The church forms, grows, suffers, triumphs, draws into its circle of creative love its worst enemy to become its greatest missionary. It is a story of continuous and rising excitement.

Many of the adventures of the intrepid Paul are told again in language concrete and graphic. One in particular is so realistically described that it is considered the most detailed account of a storm at sea and of shipwreck in any ancient literature. Luke uses the first-person technique, including himself as a companion of Paul in the experience. And certainly the authentic details confirm that the writer was an eyewitness.

It is a dramatic story. Paul, a prisoner bound for Rome, warns the Roman officer of the dangers to be encountered if they sail from Fair Havens on the isle of Crete. Ignoring his advice, the captain sets sail along the coast for a better harbor in which to winter. But a terrible Northeaster strikes and the ship is driven helplessly before it. In the lee of a small island, they hoist the boat and tie ropes around the ship in an effort to hold it together. They begin to toss the cargo overboard, and even the ship's gear and tackle.

For days and nights neither sun nor stars can be seen. The tempest howls with unabated fury. Paul comes before the company with a message from God to encourage them. After two weeks of being whirled about in blasts of wind and torrents of water, in scudding darkness and gloom, the sailors suspect they are nearing land. They drop four anchors from the stern and pray for daylight.

Paul, the prisoner, actually takes charge of the ship. He prevents the sailors from escaping in the boat; he encourages the company to have some food, and they throw the rest of the cargo into the sea. When dawn comes, they see a bay with a beach ahead and cut off the anchors, hoist what is left of the foresail, and make for the beach. The bow strikes a reef. The stern, pounded by surf, begins to break up. Then some swimming, some on planks and pieces of the ship, they all escape to the island of Malta. And from this adventure, Paul eventually is conveyed safely to Rome and to the final act in his mission to the Empire.

Drama

No perceptive reader can escape the dramatic power of such stories in the Bible. The writers had a fine feeling for the dramatic and were able to communicate scene and action unforgettably. But, strangely, the Hebrews never developed drama as such. Unlike the Greeks, they never wrote plays or built theatres for their production.

No doubt the mighty drama of the Temple liturgy, the sacrifice at the altar, the singing and the trumpets of the Levites, the marching and dancing, satisfied to some extent the basic urge for drama in the human spirit. It was out of such religious rites that Greek drama arose. But the Hebrews never bore out that development as did the later medieval church.

However, drama is implicit in many of the biblical stories. Actually, the story of the rise and fall of Saul, Israel's first king, is a tragedy in the Greek sense. If one reads it entirely, he can see the acts of a play. He detects in the character of a great man a fatal flaw (called *hubris* by the Greeks) which overwhelms him and brings him to tragic failure.

Probably the book of Job comes closest of any book in the Bible to what we mean by drama. Between the narrative prologue and the epilogue the action is carried forward almost entirely in dialogue, which is the technique of the play. But it remains basically the dialogue of discussion and does not move dramatically as drama should in order to be effective. Nevertheless, it contains poetry of the highest majesty and order. Some think it is the finest in the Bible. Since it is esentially poetry, it will be referred to again and more particularly in the next chapter, where we will consider poetic forms.

In summary, then, we can say that the Bible is unsurpassed in the brilliance, concreteness, variety, and dramatic intensity of its narratives. Read not only for their moral and spiritual value, they can give us pleasure when we re-read them as tales equal of any in the world's literature.

7.
The Bible Communicates Through Poetry

J. Wesley Ingles

Prose is an earthy, realistic sort of verbal container for ideas and human experience, as we have tried to show. In Paul's words about the preservation and communication of the gospel, "We have this treasure in earthen vessels" (2 Cor. 4:7). He was referring to our human limitations.

Poetry, however, is a finer and more artistic vessel. It is not only composed of richer material, but it is more carefully wrought. It is more obviously a work of art. It is, as someone has said, the best words in the best order. Or, as one of the proverbs puts it, "A word fitly spoken is like apples of gold in baskets of silver" (Prov. 25:11).

The proverb illustrates a basic device of poetry. It is figurative rather than literal. It appeals to the imagination of the reader or hearer, stimulating him to make comparisons, to see relationships between things not usually associated in the mind.

Elements of Poetry

Imagery

First, then, to appreciate poetry at all, and hence the poetry of the Bible, one must recognize that it is a figurative, nonliteral way of expressing ideas. Perhaps this distinction can be best understood by comparing the contrasted styles and techniques of the books of Acts and Revelation.

The former, as we noted in the previous chapter, is a masterful narration of events in the early history of the church and in the lives of its first dynamic leaders. In this historical account events are narrated in the graphic and concrete terms of the best prose. It is a literal recounting of what happened, although some of the events pass beyond our present understanding of phenomena and partake of what we call the supernatural. Even these are recounted in terms that are intended to be taken literally.

However, the book of Revelation presents a completely different literary world. This is the world of the imagination, of strange and fantastic images and vast symbols that convey truth but are not to be taken literally. Suppose one tried to draw or paint a portrait of the risen and glorified Lord as seen by John in the vision described in the opening chapter: one like a son of man, wearing a long robe with a golden girdle, his head covered with snow-white hair, and his eyes like flaming fire, with seven stars in his right hand and a sharp sword issuing from his mouth, and his face shining like the sun. This is an attempt of the poetic imagination to catch in language a vision made up of symbolic elements rather than literal and physical details. It is concrete in its imagery like the best prose, but it is highly figurative, appealing to the imagination rather than to the reason. This portrait suggests the brightness of transcendent power and glory.

And so it goes throughout the rest of the book. The magnificent pageant moves in the realms of fantasy, but it foretells the fate of men and nations. Scenes of wonder and horror pass before us. There are thrones flashing with lightnings above a sea of glass; there are living creatures full of eyes and of various shapes; there are scrolls and vials and bowls and censers and harps and voices and trumpets and thunder; horses of various colors trample across the horizon bearing strange riders; there are locusts and scorpions, devastating wars and earthshaking catastrophes, woes and anguish, darkness, destruction, and death.

But there is also an account of a final battle and a final victory. And there are choirs singing songs of adoration and praise, like the sound of many waters and reverberating thunder. The voice is that of a great multitude redeemed out of every race and nation, singing the song of triumph of the King of kings, the Lord of lords.

And there is a great city coming down out of heaven, and the rulers of the earth bring their glory into it, and its gates are never shut. And there is a river of the water of Life flowing through the middle of the city; and, on either side of the river, there is a tree of Life, bearing twelve kinds of fruit, and its leaves are for the healing of the nations. And for the redeemed inhabitants there is no night, no sorrow, no weeping, no sickness, no death. The Lord God is their light forever.

This is one majestic type of poetry, moving from the realm of the seen and the known into the realm of the unseen and the unknown, where the clash of mighty events and spiritual forces takes place behind the curtain on which flicker the shadows of the world we think of as the real. We are caught up by the imaginative sweep of this prose-poem into a world that our eyes have not seen nor our ears heard.

So, this great work illustrates one of the essentials of poetry to which we must become sensitive if we would appreciate it, that is *imagery,* appealing to the imagination. And imagery, as we shall see, involves many kinds of figures of speech and all sorts of symbols.

Rhythm

But poetry is not only the language of the imagination; it is also the language of the emotions. It is essentially the emotional response to experience expressed in cadenced speech. It is not primarily intended to convey information but to share experience.

In poetry, words are heated to a new intensity. They glow and burn. T. S. Eliot, one of the most influential poets of our century, gave us a good short definition of poetry. He called it "thought felt." And this feeling, this emotion, that pulses in poetry is conveyed through rhythm, the other essential of poetry.

Rhythm is a basic element in all life. Our breathing maintains a regular rhythmic pattern. Our heart beats its muffled drum. When these organs are functioning normally, we are hardly aware of the rhythmical patterns that sustain our life. But under the stress of emotion, the pattern of each is quickened and we become aware of it. We breathe faster and the heart drums louder.

So language tends to become more noticeably rhythmical under emotional stress. For instance, hear the heartbreaking cadence of the language in which David cries out his lament over the news that his rebellious son Absalom has been slain: "O my son Absalom, my son, my son Absalom! Would I had died instead of you, O Absalom, my son, my son!" Even though not in traditional poetic form, the rhythm and emotion are obvious.

All true poetry should be read aloud if we are to hear its cadences. And if we read this lament aloud, we cannot help feeling the passionate grief that is shaking the old king, the anguish of a father whose son has gone astray and come to a bad end.

If we observe this brief outburst, we will note that the words fall into repetitive patterns and that the pattern is reversed the second time. Here David was not composing a psalm as he had done so often in earlier years. This pattern was perfectly natural. It burst from his heart as does the agonized Irish speech of the bereaved mother in Synge's *Riders to the Sea.*

Unfortunately those of us brought up in the English-speaking tradition have come to think of meter (by which we mean language in regular patterns of accented and unaccented syllables) as essential to poetic rhythm. But this is not at all the basis of rhythm in Hebrew poetry. It is important to recognize that in the middle of the nineteenth century Walt Whitman helped to restore poetry in English to the true bases of poetic rhythms which characterized Hebrew poetry: the use of repetition of phrase and parallelism of structure and recurring sound effects.

Perhaps we can best recognize the difference between meter, a regular rhythm based on accented syllables, and the freer rhythms based on parallelism and repetition if we compare the old Scottish version of the twenty-third Psalm with the form so well known and so well loved in the King James Version. Here is what we find in the old Scots hymnal:

> The Lord's my shepherd, I'll not want,
>   He makes me down to lie
> In pastures green; He leadeth me
>   The quiet waters by.

> My soul He doth restore again,
>   And me to walk doth make
> Within the paths of righteousness
>   Ev'n for His own name's sake.

The strictures of rhyme and meter have forced the lovely cadences of the original into an almost mechanical pattern that can be sung in several verses to the same tune. But hear again the great natural rhythms of the Hebrew as caught in the Revised Standard Version, which preserves the literary values of the King James:

> The Lord is my shepherd, I shall not want;
>   he makes me lie down in green pastures.
> He leads me beside still waters;
>   he restores my soul.

He leads me in paths of righteousness
for his name's sake.

This best-loved psalm illustrates perfectly the fusion of the two essentials of all poetry: rhythm and imagery. Repetition of phrase and parallelisms of structure recur throughout the psalm, and this rhythm conveys the deep feeling of the poet about his sense of God's sustaining presence.

But the poem is based also on a series of images and symbols that are nonliteral. There are two basic metaphors: the shepherd and his sheep in the first few lines, and the king and his faithful soldier in the last few.

The green pastures and the still waters can certainly not be taken literally. Nor can they even be symbols of the external life of the poet-king, for David's outer life was surely turbulent enough. But the figure refers to the inner life, the peace which God can give to those who sense his sustaining grace and live in his presence.

There could hardly be a better figure than "the valley of the shadow" to suggest the ultimate experience of death which each must face and its imminent danger which some may time and again confront. The whole experience is imaged forth in this graphic metaphor. And what could be more suggestive of abundant blessing than an overflowing cup and a table spread with good things after a great struggle and a great victory?

This is the way poetry is made and this is the way it functions, stimulating our imagination with fresh and lovely images and moving our emotions with cadences adapted to the experiences or insights being shared by the poet.

Primitive Poetry

Actually, poetry is the oldest type of literature, and we find remnants of its earliest forms embedded in the narrative and historical books of the Bible. These were family, tribal, or folk songs of various sorts, generally composed spontaneously for some special occasion. At first they were transmitted orally from one generation to another. They probably passed through various versions before they were finally fixed and transcribed in written form.

For instance, one of these recorded in Genesis 49 is an account of Jacob pronouncing judgment upon his twelve sons before his death.

In the form of a poetic chant, each of the sons is characterized as a man and as a progenitor of a tribe. The pronouncements fall into three groups. There is condemnation on Reuben, and on Simeon and Levi. There is a measure of commendation and the prediction of a measure of good for many of the other sons. But the chief blessings are reserved for Judah and Joseph. The prophetic passages concerning their future seem to have Messianic overtones:

> The scepter shall not depart from Judah,
>> nor the ruler's staff from between his feet,
> until he comes to whom it belongs;
>> And to him shall be the obedience of the peoples.

Already one senses in these lines the rhythmical parallelism and repetition which were to become characteristics of Hebrew poetry. And in the more familiar passage on Joseph, one recognizes most richly the strong and varied imagery that runs through the whole chant:

> Joseph is a fruitful bough,
>> a fruitful bough by a spring;
>> his branches run over the wall.
> The archers fiercely attacked him,
>> shot at him, and harassed him sorely;
> yet his bow remained unmoved,
>> his arms were made agile
>> by the hands of the Mighty One of Jacob.

Here, and throughout the primitive song, one can see already the strength of the metaphor, a favorite device of Hebrew poets, as it is basic to all good poetry. One should remember that the *simile* is a stated comparison, using the signs "like" or "as" to suggest similarity as in "He eats *like* a pig." But the *metaphor* is an implied comparison as in "He *is* a pig!" It is a much stronger form of figurative language. It says or suggests that something *is* another thing, which we know it *is not* literally.

It is absolutely imperative that the reader who wishes to respond properly to this significant literary device learn to recognize its use and to distinguish the metaphoric from the literal statement. No one supposes that when Jesus said "I am the door," we are to understand that he is literally a *door*. Again when he said, "I am the good shepherd," we know that he is using "shepherd" figuratively, as was David in the twenty-third Psalm when he wrote, "The Lord is my shepherd." But, ironically and tragically, one of the major sources of division within Christendom is preserved partly by a failure to distinguish the literal from the metaphorical in a similar statement by our Lord. When he said of the paschal bread, "This is my body," it is obvious to most Reformed and Protestant Christians that he was using a metaphor, not to be taken literally. Indeed, while he said it, his hands, a part of his literal body, were quite clearly distinguishable from the pieces of bread which his hands held out to them. And yet the sacrifice of the Roman Catholic Mass is based on the conviction that these words of our Lord are to be taken literally—that the transubstantiated wafer becomes literally his body.

Who would imagine that so much might depend upon the recognition and interpretation of a metaphor? And yet there are Protestant literalists who do much the same with other metaphors in Scripture. For instance, there are some who would interpret literally the awful ills to befall the earth as announced by the trumpets of doom in Revelation 8. They would assume that, when the second angel blows his trumpet, and "something like a great mountain, burning with fire, is thrown into the sea," then a third of the sea "becomes blood"— literally. Now in our time we may begin to recognize with horror the possibility of a suggestion here of an atomic explosion ("a mountain burning with fire"), but is the one-third of the sea turned to blood to be considered literal hemoglobin? This is the disastrous literalism that cannot recognize the metaphor; a metaphor probably intended to suggest either the appearance of the destructive cataclysm or the extent of the destruction in human lives.

So the recognition and understanding of poetic language and poetic devices in the Scriptures may have significant theological implications beyond the imaginative insights and emotional impact they are intended to convey.

But to return to primitive Hebrew poetry, we may note the swan songs attributed to the aged Moses before his death as examples of the way in which great events were recreated and preserved in poetry. Judgment and blessing, warning and hope were uttered in image and cadence. Words had wings and hovered over the people and sang in the trees about them. Some of these words still sing in our ears and strengthen our hearts:

> The eternal God is your dwelling place,
>   and underneath are the everlasting arms.

The metaphor is anthropomorphic, certainly; that is, characteristics of man are attributed to God. It is not to be taken literally, but that does not mean it is not to be taken seriously. Multitudes have felt beneath them, supporting them in hours of crisis, the sustaining grace and strength of "the everlasting arms." Let theologian and philosopher rationalize the experience in intellectual abstractions. They should remember that philosophical terms are also symbolic, just as representative as mathematical figures, and for most men quite as inadequate to lift the human spirit. But the poet's metaphor in this verse, so human and yet so transcendent, can speak to our condition and meet our spiritual needs.

There is no powerful emotion, from exultation and delight to grief and bitter anguish, which cannot be rendered best in poetry. Strangely, some of the most memorable poems rise out of grief, as we saw earlier in David's passionate outburst of grief for his stricken son Absalom. A much fuller expression of this emotion is David's youthful lament for the death of Saul and Jonathan, David's best friend. Here the grief is caught in words that quiver like an unquenchable flame above a tomb. Here we can observe the effects of the moving cadences and the lovely images upon us:

Thy glory, O Israel, is slain upon thy high places!
How are the mighty fallen!

(The third line is to become a haunting refrain in the elegy.)

Tell it not in Gath,
publish it not in the streets of Ashkelon;
lest the daughters of the Philistines rejoice,
lest the daughters of the uncircumcised exult.

Ye mountains of Gilboa,
let there be no dew or rain upon you,
nor upsurging of the deep!
For there the shield of the mighty was defiled,
the shield of Saul, not anointed with oil.

From the blood of the slain,
from the fat of the mighty,
The bow of Jonathan turned not back,
and the sword of Saul returned not empty.

Saul and Jonathan, beloved and lovely!
In life and in death they were not divided;
they were swifter than eagles,
they were stronger than lions.

Ye daughters of Israel, weep over Saul,
    who clothed you daintily in scarlet,
    who put ornaments of gold upon your apparel.

How are the mighty fallen,
    in the midst of the battle!

Jonathan lies slain upon thy high places.

    I am distressed for you, my brother Jonathan;
very pleasant have you been to me;
    your love to me was wonderful,
    passing the love of women.

How are the mighty fallen,
    and the weapons of war perished!

In addition to the obvious and lovely parallelisms within the verses, there is a more subtle relationship between two of the verses; between the apostrophe [1] which calls on the mountains of Gilboa to withhold their dew and rain, and the apostrophe to the daughters of Israel to weep for Saul, to release the fountain of tears.

It is thought by some scholars that the single stark line,

    "Jonathan lies slain upon thy high places"

is really incomplete, a fragment of a couplet, but it would seem to stand poetically by itself, compelling our compassion by its powerful simplicity and restraint.

The Psalms

There are many other primitive songs embedded in the historical books, but we may observe the development of Hebrew poetry by moving from this early elegy of David's to the Psalms, so many of which are attributed to him. This has become historically the basic hymnbook and prayer book, not only of Israel but of churches of all faiths. It is an anthology of religious lyrical poetry without equal for variety and beauty in the literature of the ancient world, and it has such universal qualities that it still expresses our deepest religious emotions and touches our most vital spiritual experiences.

We can study the themes and emotions embodied in the most

---

[1] Apostrophe, as it is used here, means "words addressed to a person or thing, whether absent or present, generally in an exclamatory tone and as a digression in a speech or literary writing," according to *Webster's New World Dictionary.*

familiar and beloved psalms. We can study also the variety of song and prayer, the backgrounds out of which they were composed, and the functions they performed historically in Israel's worship. But for our devotional growth, there is probably no more rewarding type of study than literary analysis and appreciation, noting the poetic devices used and the structure of each lyric.

Take, for example, Psalm 139. Does the reader notice the striking relationship between the opening and closing verses of the psalm? It begins with reference to a great spiritual experience in the poet's past, "O Lord, thou hast searched me and known me!" and it ends with a prayer:

> Search me, O God, and know my heart!
> Try me and know my thoughts!
> And see if there be any wicked [hurtful] way in me,
> and lead me in the way everlasting!

How significant is the insight between the relationship of the opening and closing verses to the believing heart! We realize that it is not enough to have had once a great searching of soul. It is not enough to have had once the searchlight of the Holy Spirit turned upon our inmost thoughts and motives, our secret as well as our public sins. We recognize that we must seek repeatedly the *correction* of the Spirit if we would have his *direction*. It is only as God cleanses our hearts and purifies our thoughts that he can lead us in the way everlasting. So we see that a thoughtful examination of the rounded, circular form of the psalm provides a profound spiritual insight which we might have missed had we not noted this aspect of its structure.

But of course there is much more in this psalm. It centers on the realization that we can never escape the presence of the God who is everywhere. This sense of God's omnipresence makes the poet painfully aware that his failures and sins are all open to the eye of the all-seeing Judge. On the other hand, there is the comforting assurance that no matter where he may be or how lonely, abandoned, or desperate his situation, he can be aware of the divine grace, comforting, sustaining, and strengthening him. The psalm contains one of the most beautiful expressions of this concept ever written:

> Whither shall I go from thy Spirit?
> Or whither shall I flee from thy presence?
> If I ascend to heaven, thou art there!
> If I make my bed in Sheol, thou art there!

If I take the wings of the morning
    and dwell in the uttermost parts of the sea,
even there thy hand shall lead me,
    and thy right hand shall hold me.

Not only may hidden treasure thus be uncovered when we analyze the structure of any significant literary work, particularly lyrical poetry, but we may be delivered from the dangerous errors that arise from excerpting lines and passages from their context. A dramatic example of this sort of error can be seen in Thomas Paine's reference to Psalm 19 in his famous deistic work, *The Age of Reason.* He claims that this psalm and some chapters in Job are "True deistical compositions, for they treat of the Deity through his works. They take the book of Creation as the word of God. They refer to no other book." He then quotes Addison's great English hymn, based on the first six verses of Psalm 19, as evidence that the knowledge of God in nature alone provides an adequate revelation for man. This, of course, completely distorts the message of the psalm which breaks beautifully into two balanced parts. The first six verses do proclaim in majestic poetry the glory of God revealed in the physical universe, but the next seven verses proclaim in cadenced parallelism the moral law of God for man revealed by his Spirit (not to be discovered in nature!):

The law of the Lord is perfect,
    reviving the soul;
the testimony of the Lord is sure,
    making wise the simple;
the precepts of the Lord are right,
    rejoicing the heart;
the commandment of the Lord is pure,
    enlightening the eyes;
the fear of the Lord is clean,
    enduring for ever;
the ordinances of the Lord are true,
    and righteous altogether.

And here the poet uses two similes to suggest how precious and delightful to him are his meditations on the revelation of God in the written Word:

More to be desired are they than gold,
    even much fine gold;
sweeter also than honey
    and drippings of the honeycomb.

From a study of the whole psalm, we can see how important it is to recognize the various aspects of God's revelation, in Nature *and* in the written Word; and supremely, for us who can go beyond the psalmist in subsequent revelation, in the Living Word, God's Son.

The closing words of the psalm are a most fitting prayer for anyone who comes to the written revelation for guidance and strength or who desires to communicate it:

> Let the words of my mouth and the meditation of my heart
> be acceptable in thy sight,
> O Lord, my rock and my redeemer.

The Psalms have always been the devotional heart of the Scriptures, and the beauty of their imagery, the music of their cadences, and the variety of their forms will freshly and continually enrich those who meditate on them.

The Proverbs

The Proverbs, however, are in the area between prose and poetry. The subject matter, though generally prosaic and practical, is often expressed in lines that are poetic. They form a collection of wise sayings, prudential observations about life and conduct. They are basically concerned about morality and ethics, but they often rise from the quite humble and plain discussion of practical concerns to passages of wisdom expressed in the richest sort of poetic embroidery.

The poetic qualities in some passages of the Proverbs may well be illustrated in the contrasted portraits of the evil woman who lures men to destruction (chapter 6) and the noble wife and mother who is a blessing to all (chapter 31). It is a sharp contrast indeed. First the sensual woman:

> Do not desire her beauty in your heart,
> and do not let her capture you with her eyelashes;
> for a harlot may be hired for a loaf of bread,
> but an adulteress stalks a man's very life.
> Can a man carry fire in his bosom
> and his clothes not be burned?
> Or can one walk on hot coals
> and his feet not be scorched?

Then the true wife and mother:

> Strength and dignity are her clothing,
> and she laughs at the time to come.

> She opens her mouth with wisdom,
>> and the teaching of kindness is on her tongue.
> She looks well to the ways of her household,
>> and does not eat the bread of idleness.
> Her children rise up and called her blessed;
>> her husband also, and he praises her.

. . . .

> Charm is deceitful, and beauty is vain,
>> but a woman who fears the Lord is to be praised.

Probably we can also illustrate from the Proverbs most clearly (for examples abound throughout), the three basic types of parallelism in Hebrew poetry. In chapter 22 one can see all three types in the first three verses.

There is *synonymous* parallelism in which the same idea is repeated in successive lines with a slight variation of phrase:

> A good name is to be chosen rather than great riches,
>> and favor is better than silver or gold.

There is *synthetic* parallelism in which the second line amplifies, interprets, develops, or comments on the first:

> The rich and the poor meet together;
>> the Lord is the maker of them all.

And there is *antithetic* parallelism in which the second line is contrasted with, opposed to the first, sometimes ironically:

> A prudent man sees danger and hides himself;
>> but the simple go on, and suffer for it.

Sometimes the contrast is varied by reversing elements in the two lines, as in verse 7:

> The rich man rules over the poor,
>> and the borrower is the slave of the lender.

In the Proverbs, wisdom speaks in a noble voice, and those with ears will hear and give heed and will come to dwell in the House of Seven Pillars (Prov. 9:1).

Ecclesiastes and the Song of Songs

Ecclesiastes is a brilliant essay on the vanities for which so many sell their souls. It is filled with a weariness of this world, the disillusionment of a man who has tried everything and found it wanting. He has found nothing new under the sun. It is written chiefly in prose, but it contains some lovely poetry such as the catalog of the times and seasons for everything under heaven. And it ends with one of the most moving portraits of old age in all literature.

Here in chapter 12 the effects are achieved almost entirely by symbols and metaphors: the trembling keepers of the house, the strong legs bowed, the teeth decaying, the eyesight growing dim ("and those that look through the windows are dimmed"); the hearing begins to fade (sounds are low); sleep is shortened ("one rises up at the voice of a bird"); the slightest hill presents difficulties; the hair turns white ("the almond tree blossoms"); and even a "grasshopper drags itself along" and "desire fails." And approaching death is announced in the most beautiful quatrain ever written to describe it, matchless in its series of images:

> Before the silver cord is snapped,
> Or the golden bowl is broken,
> Or the pitcher is broken at the fountain,
> Or the wheel broken at the cistern,

And it goes on to its perfect consummation:

> And the dust returns to the earth as it was,
> And the spirit returns to God who gave it.

To balance the cynicism and weariness of Ecclesiastes, we should read The Song of Songs, one of the most sensitive and passionate love poems ever written. No book in the biblical canon has raised so many questions about its inclusion, or so many eyebrows about its subject matter, or so many problems of critical analysis and interpretation as this little idyll. It is a lyrical drama in which the story is merely suggested in the lyrics. Unfortunately, they are not all in the proper order, and the story has to be reconstructed, but it would seem to be about a beautiful maiden who is taken from the vineyards of Etam, south of Jerusalem, and from her beloved shepherd to the king's harem. Amid the splendor of the court and under the seductive blandishments of the king, Shelomith remains true to her beloved and is eventually restored to him.

The dramatic poem has been considered symbolic by pious and allegorizing scholars of both the Hebrew and the Christian faiths. Jews see it as an allegory of God's love for his people Israel, and

Christians see it as an allegory of the love of Christ for his espoused bride, the Church. No doubt these interpretations were given to explain the inclusion of this passionate and sensuous work in the canon. Sometimes they have been developed to the most ridiculous extremes. But actually these symbolic meanings are not necessary to justify the poem. It is the finest expression of the monogamous ideal, the union both physical and spiritual of two persons, as contrasted with the frustrating and depersonalizing elements in the polygamous relationships of the harem. It is a glorious paean to enduring love between a man and a woman:

> Set me as a seal upon your heart,
>   as a seal upon your arm;
> for love is strong as death,
>   jealousy is cruel as the grave.
> It flashes are flashes of fire,
>   a most vehement flame.
> Many waters cannot quench love,
>   neither can floods drown it.

In an age when people tend to think of sex in terms of extremes, either of prudery or of pruriency, it is important to remember that within the Scriptures the powerful force of sexual love is handled in this lovely work with unashamed realism and with unsullied idealism. This is apparently God's intention in creating man male and female, to glory in each other and to glorify the One who made them.

Dramatic Dialogue

But, loaded with magnificent imagery as is the lyrical idyll, The Song of Songs, we have not yet reached the highest levels of biblical poetry. Those levels, cloud-capped peaks, with thunderings like the voice from Sinai, are to be found in the dramatic dialogues in Job, in Isaiah, and in the lesser prophets.

Job. Out of the anguished suffering of the human spirit, some of the most profound questions are raised in the book of Job. Almost every rhetorical device is used to lift these questions into the high court of lofty discussion. Repetition builds its altar stairs toward God. In chapter 31, seventeen times the word "if" begins a phrase or sentence in Job's examination of his past life. Questions are piled one upon another, and God's answer to Job's questions is nothing but another series of magnificent questions. The ultimate limitations of human knowledge are spread before us, reducing our human pride to ashes. With Job, if we are wise, we learn to trust where we cannot know. This is certainly one of the great dramatic poems of all literature. A repeated reading of it can only help to increase our appreciation of its grand style so perfectly appropriate to the grandeur of its themes.

Isaiah. And so it is with Isaiah, in some respects the high water mark of Hebrew poetry. This is not the place to discuss the problems of authorship, whether the sixty-six chapters as we have them are the work of one author, or two or even three authors. The book obviously divides into two main sections, beginning a new tone and style with chapter 40. However, this critical question aside, we have in the complete work a consummate literary masterpiece. Of its greatness Moulton writes: "Even in literary form the world has produced nothing greater than *Isaiah* . . . But when we proceed to the matter and thought of *Isaiah* . . . how can we explain the neglect of such a masterpiece in our plans of liberal education?" [1]

Artistically, the work is rich in its combination of styles adjusted to every shade and nuance of meaning. It has the earthy concreteness characteristic of biblical prose at its best. But it is essentially poetry, using almost every literary device: hyperbole, antithesis, repetition, refrain, parable, to name only a few. It has fresh and varied imagery, cadences of melodic beauty and surging rhythms of vigorous power, impassioned eloquence, and bitter invective. Frequently, as in Job, rhetorical questions mount in dramatic sequence, beating like waves on the rocky hearts of hearers or readers. Sometimes, on the other hand, there is the quiet pastoral simplicity of still waters flowing. But nearly everywhere one feels a sublimity and grandeur adapted to and deriving from its majestic themes. "Nowhere else," writes Moulton again, "have so many colossally great ideas been brought together in a single work." [2]

Surely the greatest chapter in this great work is the famous fifty-third. By looking more closely at the literary structure of this passage we can observe again how a literary approach to great poetic passages illuminates their meaning. Also, it will help us to appreciate the vision and to share the profound emotion that were moving the prophet. He could only imagine vaguely the meaning of the awful sight of the Suffering Servant; but we, looking back through it to the cross, may sense afresh what it cost our Lord to redeem us.

---

[1] Moulton, *op. cit.,*
[2] *Ibid.*

The figure portrayed here could hardly be a symbolic representation of the Jewish people (as some of them still believe and as some critics still suggest), for this Suffering Servant is an individual. He suffers not for his own sins but for the sins of others (for the transgressions of the prophet's people). Indeed, the prophet says that he "makes himself an offering for sin."

The poem of the Suffering Servant, like Bach's great choral, "O Sacred Head Now Wounded," expresses all the anguished passion of our Lord's sacrifice. It begins with a description of the Man of Sorrows. Some, not noting that the passage should begin with verse 13 of chapter 52, have misread the reference to the Servant's lack of beauty and comeliness to mean that Jesus, like Socrates, was homely, unattractive in physical appearance. Nothing could be more erroneous. We learn from the Gospels that children ran to him eagerly, that men admired and followed him, and that women were devoted to him. When we look back to the verses at the end of chapter 52, we read that his "appearance was *marred* beyond human semblance, and his form beyond that of the sons of men." Then we compare this with earlier passages in chapter 49, where the "Redeemer of Israel" and God's "Holy One" is said to be "deeply despised, abhorred," and with chapter 50, where the cause of the marring is made more explicit:

> I gave my back to the smiters,
>   and my cheeks to those who pulled out the beard;
> I hid not my face
>   from shame and spitting.

Looking back to the focal point in history to which the prophet looked forward, we can recognize that this is an almost incredible prevision of the crucifixion (as in Psalm 22) even before that horribly shameful mode of torture and execution was invented. It is a heart-breaking description of our Lord's agony and shame:

> He was despised and rejected by men,
>   a man of sorrows, and acquainted with grief;
> and as one from whom men hide their faces
>   he was despised, and we esteemed him not.

Then the prophet, moved by the Spirit, describes the vicarious and redemptive nature of the Servant's sufferings:

> Surely *he* has borne *our* griefs
> and carried *our* sorrows;
> yet *we* esteemed *him* stricken,
> smitten by God, and afflicted.
> But *he* was wounded for *our* transgressions,
> *he* was bruised for *our* iniquities;
> upon *him* was the chastisement that made *us* whole,
> and with *his* stripes *we* are healed.
> All *we* like sheep have gone astray;
> *we* have turned every one to his own way;
> and the Lord has laid on *him*
> the iniquity of *us all.*

When this passage is read aloud, the pronouns here italicized should be accented. Only so we can feel the full force of the realization that our Lord's atoning sacrifice was for *us.* Here again it is a literary understanding that leads to theological and spiritual apprehension of the insights conveyed by the prophet.

Like the Psalms, the books of the prophets contain passages that have become part of the treasure of all true believers. The stirring outcry of their eloquent voices against injustice is balanced by the comfort of the promises of healing and renewal and strength they hold out. And as in Job, there is a stubborn and unconquerable faith in God in spite of every appearance of desertion by him. It is powerfully asserted by Habakkuk in a great periodic sentence that builds to its climax at the end, a rising crescendo of faith:

> Though the fig tree do not blossom,
> nor fruit be on the vines,
> the produce of the olive fail
> and the fields yield no food,
> the flock be cut off from the fold
> and there be no herd in the stalls,
> yet will I rejoice in the Lord,
> I will joy in the God of my salvation.

And Isaiah lifts us to the basis for that faith when he shares with us God's promise to man in his extremity:

> Fear not, for I am with you,
> be not dismayed, for I am your God;
> I will strengthen you,

I will help you,
I will uphold you
With my victorious right hand.

Poetry in the New Testament

Obviously most of the great poetry of the Bible is in the Old Testament, but there are passages that soar into poetic beauty in the New Testament as well. We have already referred at the beginning of this chapter to the great prose-poem of the book of Revelation, which most clearly resembles the poetry of the Old Testament. Indeed it is based upon and is an extension of the prophets of Israel and uses the same symbolic and metaphoric language.

But we must not forget that Paul, the learned scholar and profound theologian and intrepid missionary, was also a poet. Although his writings were essentially rational and logical, they were at times emotional and imaginative. In him, head and heart were united. As we read the closely reasoned logic of his epistle to the Romans, we should note the poetic bursts of impassioned eloquence that break out when he is moved by his theme. At the end of chapter 7, bemoaning his divided state before he found peace in Christ, Paul cries out:

Wretched man that I am!
Who will deliver me from this body of death?
Thanks be to God through Jesus Christ our Lord!

And when he comes to the end of chapter 8 about life in the Spirit and our victory in Christ, his style rises in a poetic paean that begins (like some passages in Isaiah) with a series of rhetorical questions and ends with a triumphant statement of faith:

What then shall we say to this?
If God is for us, who is against us?
He who did not spare his own Son
But gave him up for us all,
Will he not also give us all things with him?
Who shall bring any charge against God's elect?
    It is God who justifies;
Who is to condemn?
    Is it Christ Jesus, who died,
    Yes, who was raised from the dead,
    Who is at the right hand of God,
    Who indeed intercedes for us?
Who shall separate us from the love of Christ?

Shall tribulation,
Or distress,
Or persecution,
Or famine,
Or nakedness,
Or peril,
Or sword? . . . .
No, in all these things we are more than conquerors
Through him who loved us.
For I am sure that neither death,
Nor life,
Nor angels,
Nor principalities,
Nor things present,
Nor things to come,
Nor powers,
Nor height,
Nor depth,
Nor anything else in all creation,
Will be able to separate us from the love of God
In Christ Jesus our Lord.

(Both of these passages have been arranged by the writer in blank verse form to emphasize poetic character.)

His letters are full of poetic exclamations:

O the depth of the riches and wisdom and knowledge of God!

And,   O death, where is thy victory?
O death, where is thy sting?
The sting of death is sin,
And the power of sin is the law.
But thanks be to God, who gives us the victory
Through our Lord Jesus Christ.

But certainly the most beautiful poetic passage in the letters of Paul is the 13th chapter of 1 Corinthians. It is a noble poem about *agape* love, about the quality of life that the new person in Christ should reveal in all his human relationships. Just as some preachers have written hymns that will be sung after their greatest sermon may be forgotten, so Paul composed this matchless hymn of love. Its beautiful repetitions and contrasts will sing in our hearts when the most profound reaches of his logic may not move us. This is the power of poetry—to lift the human spirit and to transcend "the rude wasting of old Time."

8.
The Text and Canon of the Old Testament
Frank Stagg

As late as 1944 Sir Frederick Kenyon, for many years the director and chief librarian of the British Museum, could say, "The earliest Hebrew manuscript now known of any part of the Bible is not earlier than the ninth century after Christ." [1] His reference was to a copy of the Pentateuch (first five books of the Old Testament) in the British Museum (Or. 4445). At that time he could refer to a manuscript of the Prophets at Leningrad dated A.D. 916 or A.D. 1008 [2] and to a manuscript at Oxford, which was a copy of most of the Old Testament dating from the tenth century. There was also the Cairo Codex of the Prophets (A.D. 895). Except for a few other manuscripts of uncertain dates, including a Samaritan Pentateuch, this was about the story. Thus, more than a thousand years stood between the last written books of the Old Testament and the oldest known Hebrew manuscripts.

In 1947 Frederick C. Prussner complained that Old Testament textual criticism was all but over because the materials for recovering the original text had been exhausted; and he could only hold out "the remote hope that the discovery of new manuscripts" would clear up a few more difficulties.[3] But little did Kenyon, Prussner, or anyone else know that in 1947 there would be recovered from near the Dead Sea some ancient scrolls which would completely change this picture. The Dead Sea Scrolls include some parts of the Old Testament written in Hebrew before the birth of Christ.

In this chapter we will see some of the roads which take us back toward the "original text" of the Old Testament: Hebrew manuscripts,

---

[1] Sir Frederic Kenyon, *The Story of the Bible* (reprinted; London: John Murray, 1944), p. 11.
[2] B. J. Roberts, "Old Testament Text," *Interpreters' Dictionary of the Bible*, IV, p. 588.
[3] Frederick C. Prussner, "Problems Ahead in Old Testament Research," *The Study of the Bible Today and Tomorrow* (Chicago: U. G. Chicago Press, 1947), pp. 179 f.

Greek translations of the Old Testament, and the Samaritan Bible. The span of centuries is greater and the materials are fewer for the Old Testament text than for the New. It does not necessarily follow that the text of the Old Testament is less certain than that of the New. The original text of neither has been fully recovered, yet a reasonably accurate reconstruction of each text is possible. From existing manuscripts, scholars keep moving upstream to the fountain heads.

The Masoretic Hebrew Text

The text of the Hebrew Bible has come down to the present time with little traceable change since about A.D. 100. What is known as the Masoretic text was almost universally accepted through that period. *Masora* is the Hebrew word for tradition. The Masoretic text is thus the traditional text for the Hebrew Bible. In like manner the Vulgate became the generally accepted text for the Latin Bible and the Textus Receptus (Received Text) became the generally accepted text for the Greek New Testament following the work of Erasmus.

The Masoretic text emerged from the period which followed the first Jewish-Roman War (A.D. 66-70). In A.D. 70 the Romans under Titus, later to become Emperor, broke through the walls of Jerusalem and destroyed the city. The Temple was destroyed and has never been rebuilt, so all the work of the priests came to an end. The Sadducees disappeared from the scene along with the whole cultic practice which depended upon the Temple. The Pharisees emerged as the unrivaled leaders of the Jewish people and greater attention than ever was given to the Scriptures and the synagogue. The Pharisaic center was moved to the town of Jamnia (Yabneh), where study and teaching centered in "the Law" as contained in the Scriptures. Rabbi Akiba was the most influential rabbi from the destruction of Jerusalem until the outbreak of the Second Jewish War (A.D. 132-135). During this time a standardized text of the Hebrew Bible was adopted by the Jews. Either a standard text was produced out of the various existing texts or the Pharisees adopted a text already standardized. There is evidence from a scroll of Isaiah (1 QIs [b]), one of the Dead Sea Scrolls found at Qumran, for a type of Hebrew text already standardized before the time of the Masoretes and perpetuated rather than created by the Masoretes.[4]

---

[4]Roberts, *op. cit.*, p. 582.

Roads Back to the Old Testament Text

There is more material for testing or recovering the test of the
Old Testament today than has been true for nearly two thousand
years. There are recent manuscript discoveries which reach far deeper
into the past than was true even several decades ago.

The Cairo Genizah. In 1890 an old synagogue in Cairo dating from
A.D. 882 was rebuilt, and many thousands of fragments of manuscripts
in its genizah (storeroom) became accessible to scholars. A genizah
is a storeroom in a synagogue to which are consigned sacred texts
no longer usable or heretical texts. In the Cairo genizah were found
about a quarter of a million fragments of biblical and other texts
in Hebrew, Aramaic, Arabic, Samaritan, and Greek.[5] Many of these
fragments are now found throughout the world, but the majority are
in the libraries of Cambridge, Oxford, Manchester, and the British
Museum. These fragments provided a basis for inquiry behind the
Masoretic text and led some scholars to the conclusion that there
were two ancient Hebrew textual traditions, one Babylonian and one
Palestinian.[6]

The Dead Sea Scrolls. Since 1947 many manuscripts have been
recovered from caves in the vicinity of the Dead Sea. Some of the
scrolls from Qumran are about a thousand years older than any other
extant manuscript of the Hebrew Bible. One of these scrolls contains
the whole of Isaiah and a commentary on Habakkuk (1 QIs[a]). It
is now in the Hebrew University in Jerusalem, Israel. The Revised
Standard Version adopted thirteen readings from this manuscript.
Another scroll of Isaiah (1 QIs[b]) bears striking similarity to the
Masoretic text, yet it has some significant differences. These manuscripts preserve texts which were in use before the time of Christ.
Their scribes were not rigid in adhering to a standardized text. From
a cave near Qumran came a manuscript of Samuel (4 QSam[b]),
thought by some to date back to around the end of the third century
B.C. Another manuscript of Samuel (4 QSam[a]) is of similar text type.
An Exodus Scroll (4 QEx[a]) has affinities with the Samaritan Pentateuch and the Septuagint.[7] Fragments of Leviticus 19-23 survive in
a scroll written in an old script known as Paleo-Hebrew (1 QLev.).

[5] H. M. Orlinshy, "Genizah," *The Interpreter's Dictionary of the Bible,* II, p. 381.
[6] Roberts. *op. cit.,* pp. 587f.
[7] *Ibid.*

At Wadi Murabba'at were found biblical scrolls belonging to the time of the Second Jewish-Roman War (A.D. 132-35). These are closer to the Masoretic text than are the Hebrew texts found at Qumran. From a cave in this area was recovered a scroll in Greek, with fragments of the minor prophets, possibly dating from the end of the first century of the Christian era. This manuscript seems to support the view that there was a variety of texts of the Greek Bible at the beginning of the Christian era.

The Samaritan Pentateuch. Tourists who visit the small Samaritan community at Nablus are shown an old scroll of the Pentateuch which the tribal priests proudly trace back to Aaron. No scholar accepts so great an age for the scroll. However, it does preserve an ancient text, similar to an Exodus Scroll found at Qumran (4 Q EX^a). The manuscript seems to be mixed, partly ancient and a part from the fourteenth century. It has about six thousand variants from the Masoretic text, mostly in spelling but some of significance. The Samaritans recognize only the Pentateuch, reflecting the probable canon at the time of their separation from the Jews.

The Septuagint. From between 150 B.C. and 100 B.C. comes an apocryphal letter known as the *Letter of Aristeas,* addressed to Philocrates during the reign of Ptolemy Philadelphus (285-246 B.C.), King of Egypt. The letter presumes to tell of the first translation of the Hebrew Bible into Greek. The story is very dramatic but not considered authentic. In brief, it is held that seventy scholars made the translation at the request of Ptolemy Philadelphus, who wanted it for his library at Alexandria.

The story has it that Ptolemy heard about the Jewish Scriptures and sent a committee to the high priest at Jerusalem, requesting a copy of the Hebrew books for translation into Greek. The *Letter of Aristeas* has it that the high priest sent six scholars from each of the twelve tribes with a copy of the Law written in letters of gold. They were given a banquet, displayed their wisdom, and were assigned quarters on the Island of Pharos. In seventy-two days the seventy-two men are said to have completed their task. The translation was pronounced perfect, and a curse was levied upon anyone who should make any change in it. The name Septuagint (LXX) derives from the story of the seventy (—two) translators.

The *Letter of Aristeas* is thought to be apocryphal and deliberate propaganda designed to support one particular version of the Greek version of the Torah (Law).[8] The very concern of the letter is evidence that there were rival Greek versions. Most of the details in the letter may be dismissed as fiction, but some solid facts seem to emerge. By 100 B.C. there is clear evidence that Jews did use Greek in their synagogues in Alexandria, Egypt, where they constituted about two fifths of the city's population.[9] Probably at least the Torah (first five books of the Old Testament) was translated into Greek in Alexandria during the third century before Christ. Before the end of the first century B.C. all of the Jewish Scriptures were translated into Greek, and other Jewish books were written into Greek originally. The translation work was not of uniform quality, ranging from the crudely literal to paraphrase. The work was done at different times, not in seventy-two days; and more than one translator worked on each book.

Other Greek versions. The first Christians were Jews, and for a time they worshiped in the synagogues, where the Jewish Scriptures were read. Their first Bible was what we know as the Old Testament. For the most part they read the Greek version of the Jewish Scriptures. When Judaism and Christianity parted ways, Christians continued to use the Septuagint as their Bible; and they used the Septuagint to refute the Jews. It was at this point that the Jews turned from the Septuagint and prepared their own versions. Orthodox Judaism excluded the Septuagint from the synagogues, just as the church itself had been gradually pushed out.[10]

In A.D. 128 a crudely literal translation from Hebrew into Greek was made by Aquila, a proselyte to Judaism from Pontus. About A.D. 130 the Septuagint was condemned by Rabbi Akiba, and Aquila's version replaced it. About the same time Theodotian made a revision of a Greek version, bringing it into closer agreement with the Hebrew. It is not certain what Greek version he based his revision on, probably not the Septuagint. The text which Theodotian used seems to be a Greek version employed by some New Testament writers, and his version of Daniel was adopted by the church in preference to the Septuagint.[11] A third Greek version was produced about A.D. 179 by an Ebionite Christian named Symmachus. It was a free translation,

[8] F. C. Grant, *Translating the Bible* (Greenwich, Conn.: The Seabury Press, 1961), p. 21.
[9] *Ibid.*, p. 22.
[10] B. J. Roberts, "The Ancient Versions of the Old Testament," *Peake's Commentary on the Bible* (New York: Thomas Nelson and Sons, 1962), p. 81.
[11] *Ibid.*, p. 24.

the opposite to that of Aquila.

Christian revisions of the Septuagint. Beginning in the third century of the Christian era, there were several attempts by Christian scholars to restore the true text of the Old Testament. Their work served both to clarify and confuse. They provide further evidence for the ancient texts, but in their work is also a blending of old and new readings and, in effect, the production of new texts.

Origen (c. 254) is known as the father of Septuagint criticism.[12] Early in the third century he set himself to the task of trying to bring order out of the great variety of Greek versions of the Old Testament. He studied Hebrew and collected a vast amount of material. He produced a great Bible known as the Hexapla (so named because in six parallel columns it gave Hebrew and Greek versions of the Old Testament). Column one contained the Hebrew text, virtually the current Masoretic text; column two, a transliteration of the Hebrew; column three, the Greek version of Aquila; column four, the Greek version of Symmachus; column five, Origen's revision of the Septuagint; and column six, the Greek version of Theodotian. For the Psalms there were three additional texts, which he called by the Greek equivalents of Quinta (5th), Sexta (6th), and Septima (7th). Origen said the Sexta came from a cave near Jericho. Whether or not this meant Qumran or Murabba'at is not known.

Origen saw the differences between the Hebrew text and that of the Septuagint. He used a system of symbols to mark the differences, one symbol for passages in the Septuagint but not in the Hebrew and one for passages in the Hebrew but not in the Septuagint. The original manuscript of the Hexapla was kept in Caesarea. It was studied there by Jerome in the fourth century but was destroyed by the Arabs in 638. Except for column five, only fragments have survived. In 617, shortly before the Muslims destroyed the library at Caesarea, Bishop Paul of Tella in Mesopotamia translated Origen's Septuagint, retaining the valuable symbols which marked the differences between the Hebrew and Septuagint texts. An eighth-century manuscript of this work is in the possession of the Ambrosian Library in Milan, Italy.

A second revision of the Septuagint by a Christian was that made by Hesychius, a bishop in Egypt. He suffered martyrdom in A.D. 311.

---

[12] J. W. Wevers. "Septuagint." *The Interpreter's Dictionary of the Bible.* IV. p. 275.

Lucian, presbyter of Antioch, prepared a revision which was widely accepted in Asia Minor. He, too, was a martyr to the persecution of Maximus. Thus, it appears that there was not one single Septuagint text but a variety of translations and revisions which may be called the Greek Bible or Greek Old Testament.[13]

The Greek Bible was the Bible of the early church, and the Old Testament as well as the New survives in early manuscripts. One of the earliest and best manuscripts containing the Septuagint is Codex Vaticanus, property of the Vatican Library in Rome. It dates from about A.D. 350. In the British Museum is Codex Sinaiticus, another vellum manuscript of the fourth century, a little later than Codex Vaticanus. From the fifth century is another vellum manuscript now in the British Museum, Codex Alexandrinus. It too contains the Septuagint. In the National Library in Paris is Codex Ephraemi, a fifth-century palimpsest, a manuscript written over an earlier writing that had been scraped from the vellum. It, too, preserves a part of the Septuagint.

Other versions. Although the Hebrew Scriptures were first translated into Greek, they have also been translated into other versions, the Latin and Syriac being next to the Greek in importance. Coptic and Ethiopic versions are also important in the recovery of the text of the Old Testament.

Except for the Greek translations of the Hebrew Bible, probably the most significant version is the Latin Vulgate (the Old Testament portion). Although the New Testament portion of the Vulgate was inferior (being a reworking of an existing Latin version), the Old Testament Vulgate was a superior work. Jerome produced it when he lived in Palestine between A.D. 390 and 405. He learned Hebrew and translated from the Hebrew. He preferred the Hebrew over the Greek text and also the Hebrew canon over the larger Alexandrian (Septuagint) collection. Unfortunately, the text of Jerome's Vulgate has undergone considerable change, partly by the inevitable errors in transmitting from manuscript to manuscript and partly by deliberate choice on the part of those who favored the Septuagint and the Old Latin versions which he was supposedly commissioned to correct.

The Canon of the Hebrew Bible

It is somewhat misleading to speak of the Hebrew Bible in ancient

[13] Cf. Grant, *op. cit.*, p. 27.

times, for it was not until the invention of printing that the Hebrew Scriptures were gathered together in one complete book. In the time of Jesus, a synagogue would possess possibly from twelve to twenty leather scrolls, each containing one or a group of Hebrew writings.[14] The Jews did gradually arrive at a canon or list of books which were given a unique authority as their Scriptures. When finalized, the Hebrew canon consisted of the thirty-nine writings which now compose the Protestant Old Testament. However, as the Jews counted the books there were twenty-four. The books of Samuel, Kings, Chronicles, and Ezra-Nehemiah were counted as one each, hence four and not eight books; and the twelve minor prophets were counted as one book. Not only were the books of the Hebrew Bible counted differently, but their arrangement was unlike that in English Bibles.

The Hebrew canon was formed in three stages: the Law, the Prophets, and the Writings. Each stage was brought to a climax by a crisis. The overall period in which the canon took shape was from the Babylonian Exile until after the destruction of Jerusalem in A.D. 70. This does not mean that there were no writings earlier than the Exile or that some of them were as late as A.D. 70. Before 621 B.C., Israel possessed some great literature which became a part of the Hebrew canon. But it was only under the pressure of some crisis that steps were taken to draw a clear line between writings which were to be recognized as canonical and those not.

The Law. The first five books of the Hebrew Bible were called the Torah, commonly translated Law although the Hebrew word more nearly means "teaching or instruction (doctrine)." These five books are also called the Pentateuch (fivefold): Genesis, Exodus, Leviticus, Numbers, and Deuteronomy. The Babylonian Exile provided the crisis out of which the Torah won undisputed place in the faith and life of the Jews. In 621 B.C. the "book of the Law" was found in the Temple (2 Kings 22-23; 2 Chron. 34:14), and it became the basis for the reforms under Josiah and virtually constituted "Judaism" out of Israel. Scholars generally hold this book to have been Deuteronomy or the major part of it.[15] Deuteronomy represents the fusion of the great priestly and prophetic forces in Judaism.[16] Behind Deuteronomy

---

[14] E. J. Goodspeed. *How Came the Bible?* (Nashville: Abingdon-Cokesbury Press. 1940). p. 10.

[15] R. H. Pfeiffer. "Canon of the Old Testament." *The Interpreter's Dictionary of the Bible.* IV. p. 502.

[16] Goodspeed. *op. cit.,* pp. 21 f.

are probably much older Hebrew codes of law (cf. Ex. 20:22 to 23:33 and Ex. 34). Around this nucleus probably grew the Pentateuch, completed some time before the split between the Jews and the Samaritans, for the Pentateuch is the Samaritan Bible. The Sadducees, too, recognized only the Pentateuch. The Jews eventually recognized a much larger canon (Law, Prophets, and Writings), but even for them the Law was always given first rank, a kind of proto-canon (a first canon).

The Prophets. The second part of the Hebrew canon to be completed and recognized was the division known as "The Prophets," consisting of the Former Prophets (Joshua, Judges, Samuel, and Kings) and the Latter Prophets (Isaiah, Jeremiah, Ezekiel, and the twelve "Minor Prophets"). The Latter Prophets included Hosea, Joel, Amos, Obadiah, Jonah, Micah, Nahum, Habukkuk, Zephaniah, Haggai, Zechariah, and Malachi; and they were written on one scroll. The Former Prophets as well as Isaiah, Jeremiah, and Ezekiel would occupy one scroll each. The division of the Prophets was probably collected and recognized as authoritative between 250 and 175 B.C. The crisis brought upon the Jews when the Syrian King Antiochus Epiphanes (175-164 B.C.) sought to change Jews into Greeks probably was the occasion for the finalizing of this part of the canon. Antiochus singled out the sacred books of the Jews for destruction, forbidding the reading of them. This made it highly important to the Jews that they know which books were Scripture, hence which worth suffering for.[17] It is from a time shortly after that the first clear evidence comes for the canon. The prologue to the Greek translation of the Wisdom of Sirach (Ecclesiasticus), written about 130 B.C., refers to "the law and the prophets and and other ancestral books." [18] For some time the Hebrew canon consisted of the "Law and the Prophets," and this title is found in the New Testament (Cf. Matt. 5:17; 7:12; 11:13; 22:40; Luke 16:16; Acts 13:15; Rom. 3:21).

The Writings. The third collection of books to be canonized by the Jews is known as the Writings (Psalms, Proverbs, Ecclesiastes, Job, Esther, Ruth, Song of Songs, Lamentations, Daniel, Ezra, Nehemiah, and Chronicles). In Luke 24:44 there is a reference to the Law,

---

[17] E. C. Colwell, *The Study of the Bible* (Chicago: The University of Chicago Press, 1937), p. 12.

[18] Robert M. Grant, *The Formation of the New Testament* (New York: Harper and Row, 1965). p. 33.

the Prophets, and the Psalms. The Writings were headed by the Psalms, and the third unit of the Hebrew canon was sometimes referred to as "The Psalms." Probably the occasion for the closing of the destruction of Jerusalem in A.D. 70, the separation of synagogue and church, and the appearance of Christian writings. There is no evidence that the Writings were accepted by the Sadducees, who disappeared after A.D. 70. Some of the Writings were found among the Qumran Scrolls, but they were written on inferior materials and in less formal script than books of the Law and the Prophets.[19]

Canonizing acts intended not only to include but to exclude. The action at Jamnia, possible around A.D. 85-90, was designed to exclude not only Christian writings but also some Jewish books which Christians had taken over from the Jews. In this action the Jews rejected the Septuagint, the Greek Bible of the earliest Christians. The Septuagint represented the canon of Alexandrian Jews. It was larger than the Hebrew canon which was adopted under the influence of the Pharisees at Jamnia.

The earliest Jews description of the complete Hebrew canon is found in the apology of Josephus named *Against Apion* (*ca.* A.D. 94-96). He sets twenty-two dependable books over against countless discordant and conflicting ones: five books of Moses, thirteen books of the Prophets, and four books of hymns and moral precepts. He counted Ruth with Judges and Lamentations with Jeremiah, thus arriving at a total of twenty-two (the number of letters in the Hebrew alphabet) rather than twenty-four. Our thirty-nine books represents yet another way of counting the identical three-fold collection.[20]

The Alexandrian Canon: the Septuagint

The Greek Bible known as the Septuagint represents a larger canon of Scripture than the Hebrew Bible. It is not possible to narrow the Greek Bible (the Septuagint) to one fixed collection. The Pharisees at Jamnia (*ca.* 85-90) seem to have fixed the Hebrew canon, drawing a clear line between the canonical and the "outside books"; but no such action was taken to fix the limits of the Greek Bible (whether called Septuagint or Greek Old Testament). It remained fluid and open. There may not have been either a fixed collection or a stan-

---

[19] Floyd V. Filson. *Which Books Belong in the Bible?* (Philadelphia: The Westminster Press. 1957), p. 47.
[20] Cf. Robert M. Grant, *op. cit.,* pp. 34-36.

dardized Greek text for what is commonly called "the Septuagint."

The difference between the Old Testament for Protestants and that for Roman Catholics results from the difference between the Hebrew canon adopted at Jamnia by the Jews and the larger, more open and fluid Greek Bible of the Jews at Alexandria. Christians for some time employed the Greek Bible of Alexandria, even though they often recognized the distinction between it and the more restricted Hebrew canon.

Christian use of books of the Greek Bible (Septuagint) is reflected in the fact that some of them are in the oldest extant manuscripts. The Septuagint survived only through Christian copies. Codex Vaticanus (ca. 350) includes the "apocryphal" books of 1 Esdras, Wisdom of Sirach, additions to Esther, Judith, Tobit, Baruch, and the Epistle of Jeremiah. Codex Sinaiticus (ca. 375) has these same "apocryphal" books and 1 and 2 Maccabees in the Old Testament as well as the Epistle of Barnabas and the Shepherd of Hermas in the New. Codex Alexandrinus (5th century) has yet other "outside books": 3 and 4 Maccabees, Odes, Psalms of Solomon, Prayer of Manasseh, and additions to Daniel in the Old Testament as well as 1 and 2 Clement in the New. Older than these parchment (vellum) manuscripts are some on papyrus which were published in 1935 as a part of the Chester Beatty collection. The oldest is a copy of Numbers and Deuteronomy, dating from about A.D. 120-150. From the third century are large portions of Genesis, Isaiah, Ezekiel, Daniel, and Esther, and fragments of Jeremiah.[21]

Early Christians struggled over the question of which books inherited from the Jews belonged to the Bible. Bishop Melito of Sardis made a trip to Palestine to learn the number and order of the books to be included in the Old Testament. He omitted Esther, as did Athanasius in his famous Easter letter of A.D. 367, probably because it does not refer directly to God.[22] Jerome, who prepared the Latin Vulgate in the fourth century, followed the Hebrew canon and recognized the additional books of the Septuagint as only "deutero-canonical" or secondary. He was followed in this by scholars like Cardinal Cajetan, before whom Luther was summoned for trial. The Council of Trent (1545-63) ruled that the larger Septuagint collection

[21] Kenyon, op. cit., p. 14.
[22] Filson, op. cit., p. 49.

was canonical and thus closed the issue for the Roman Church.

Protestant Bibles continued to carry the "apocryphal" books until recent times. It was Luther who first separated them from the other books, putting them in a group to themselves at the end of the Old Testament in his German Bible of 1534. This pattern was followed by all of the great printed English Bibles from Coverdale (1535) through the King James (1611). A few old pulpit Bibles may yet be found in Baptist churches in the South (U.S.A.) containing the apocryphal writings at the end of the Old Testament. Some of these apocryphal books are of great historical value, for example, 1 Maccabees. Books like Judith and Tobit throw much light on pre-Christian Pharisaism. The Wisdom Literature and the Prayer of Manasseh contain some excellent insights and warm devotion. The apocryphal books are still valuable for bridging the gap between the Old Testament and the New and for a better understanding of the world into which Jesus came.

9.
The Text and Canon of the New Testament

Frank Stagg

Imagine yourself as a translator of the New Testament. You know Greek and want to translate the Greek New Testament into English. Where do you start? What Greek text do you use? The answer is not easy. The first problem is to settle on the Greek text to be followed in those places where the manuscripts differ. Every printed Greek New Testament represents a selection of readings from manuscripts which differ at many points. Behind every translation, including the King James Version, many choices of the Greek text were made. This is called textual criticism. No Bible reader escapes it. The only option one has is to accept the work of some textual critic or to learn the science and make one's own selections.

Textual criticism is the science through which attempt is made to recover the original text of any writing. If the autograph survives, there is no need for textual criticism. An autograph is the author's own original. We were tempted to say, his own original *copy;* but copy is not the word we want. Copies are never identical with that which is being copied. When any writing is reproduced, changes are made. Even in printing, there has never been a perfect copy of the author's manuscript. Before printing, when all books were handwritten (manuscript), the changes were even harder to avoid. Try it! Copy one page from a book and see how hard it is to be exact.

Not one autograph of a biblical writing has come down to us. Probably they perished at a very early period. Could he recover the autographs, the textual critic would have nothing to do. Without them his task is to compare all copies and to select the reading most likely to be the original. He does not want to add, subtract, or change one word of the Bible. He wants to discover what already has been added, subtracted, or changed so that he may get back to the original.

How Variants Arose

Of the thousands of New Testament manuscripts in Greek, Syriac, Latin, Coptic, and other languages, no two agree at every point. In fact, there are multiplied thousands of differences among them. Many of the variants are insignificant, like differences in spelling or word order. Some variants are very important. For example, in some copies the Gospel of Mark ends at 16:8. Did the original?

Since printing was unknown in Europe and the Middle East until the middle of the fifteenth century, all books prior to that were handwritten. Scribes were either amateur or professional. They wrote on papyrus or skins (called parchment or vellum). They wrote with homemade pens and ink. It is now known that scribes did not usually sit at a table to write. The scribe would write in a sitting posture, with the tablet on his knee. At night his light would come from an oil lamp. The scribe worked directly from another manuscript or wrote as another read to him. Multiple copies could be made as one read aloud and two or more scribes took down the dictation.

Errors or variants could arise if the scribe misread the text he was copying or misunderstood the reader. Ancient manuscripts had no punctuation, not even spacing between words. This added to the difficulty of correct copying. Words which looked alike or sounded alike could be confused. Similar endings of words or clauses could cause repetitions or omissions. Some changes were intentional. This was true expecially in the earliest period, before there was general agreement among Christians as to which books were canonical. Scribes sometimes tried to improve on the style of the text. Sometimes they sought to clarify difficult readings. They tended to harmonize Old and New Testament readings or one Gospel with another. Sometimes they incorporated into the biblical text what had been a comment written in the margin or between lines. For these and other reasons, variants multiplied with each copying.

Periodically there were efforts to standardize biblical texts. By the second century of the Christian era such efforts had been made by Jewish scholars for the Hebrew Old Testament. As a result the Masoretic Hebrew text was almost universally followed for centuries. No such success followed any recension (standardization) of the New Testament text. It seems that by the fourth century there had been an effort to standardize the text at Alexandria, Egypt, where Greek was the basic language of scholars. In the fourth century, the Latin Vulgate was produced as an effort to standardize older Latin versions. In the fifth century the Peshitta was a recesion designed to standardize older Syriac versions. Thus by deliberate plan or by tendencies to conform, various text types emerged. How to untangle all of this, getting behind the recensions as well as the scribal changes, is the unending task of textual criticism.

The Making of Ancient Books

Materials. The oldest known New Testament manuscripts are written on papyrus, ancestor to paper. Papyrus sheets were made from the pith of papyrus plants, found chiefly along the Nile. Strips of the centers of papyrus plants were laid lengthwise and crosswise and pressed together into sheets. It was easier to write on the strips running horizontally than on those running vertically. These sides were called recto (right side) and verso (reverse), respectively. Papyrus was less expensive than parchment, but it was also more fragile and perishable. It could survive only in a dry climate, hence most papyri known to us have been recovered from the sands of Egypt.

More substantial than papyrus are the skins of animals. The Jews required that their Scriptures be written on skins. Christians wrote their Scriptures on both papyrus and skins. Parchment is the term generally used for skins used as writing material. Strictly speaking, vellum is the term appropriate to biblical manuscripts. Vellum designated the finer grade of parchment, made from young animals (vellum and veal are from the same Latin root). The hair was removed and the skins were scraped and smoothed until paper thin, suited for writing on both sides.

Book forms. The earliest books were rolls or scrolls. For the Jewish Scriptures, scrolls were required. Probably the New Testament writings originated on papyrus and as scrolls. There was a length beyond which a scroll would become unwieldy, and this was an important factor in the maximum length for books. The codex was much more convenient and was used by Christians beginning no later than the second quarter of the second century. A codex is a book made up of leaves, like a modern book. Even so, without chapter or verse divisions and without punctuation or even spacing between words, the early codex was not so convenient as a modern book.

Style of writing. The New Testament manuscripts have come to us in both majuscule and minuscule styles of writing. Majuscule refers to the employment of large or capital letters throughout. These are sometimes called uncial, meaning inch. Except for a few ornamental letters at the beginning of a book or a section, the letters were not actually an inch high, but they were block-type or capital letters. Minuscules were small letters, written in a flowing hand, called cursive. The oldest New Testament manuscripts on vellum are uncial or majuscule. From about the ninth century the vellum manuscripts are minuscule or cursive. Papyrus has a somewhat different story, and the terms majuscule and minuscule are not usually employed for the papyrus manuscripts.

Source Materials for Textual Recovery

There are many ancient source materials out of which printed Greek Testaments are edited and out of which translations are made into modern languages. These materials consist of manuscripts in Greek, the original language of the New Testament, plus manuscripts in early translations of the Greek into Syriac, Latin, Coptic, and other languages. Quotations of passages from the New Testament in the sermons, commentaries, and other writings of the early church fathers offer another body of source material. Liturgical readings, compilations of Scriptures as in "responsive readings," offer yet another source for recovering the early New Testament text.

Greek Manuscripts. Probably the copying of the writings of the New Testament began at a very early date. Ephesians may have been sent out to various churches simultaneously. Copies were made of the originals, and copies were made from copies.

At this writing there are 76 Greek manuscripts written on papyrus, some containing only a few verses and some containing a collection of New Testament writings. There are 241 Greek New Testament manuscripts on vellum, written in capital letters (majuscules or uncial), dating from the fourth to the tenth centuries. There are 2,533 such manuscripts written in small, flowing letters (minuscule or cursive), dating from the eighth or ninth centuries to the time of printing. There are 1,838 lectionaries (collections of passages similar to responsive or liturgical readings). There are also 25 ostraca (broken pottery used for writing material) and nine talismen (amulets worn as charms) containing verses from the New Testament.[1]

Early versions. The most important versions for the recovery of the New Testament text are Syriac, Latin, and Coptic. Probably by the second century there were translations of certain New Testament writings into these languages. Syriac would have been required for many people in Syria and the Middle East. Latin translations were first required for Christians in North Africa, then in Europe. Christians in Rome seem to have spoken Greek long before they spoke Latin. In Alexandria, Egypt, Greek was the language of most Christians; but in much of Egypt, Coptic was spoken.

We do not have any of the originals in these languages, but we do have manuscripts from early times, beginning in the third century. There is a Coptic manuscript on papyrus at the University of Mississippi dating possibly from the third century and containing 1 Peter, Jonah, and other writings.

Of secondary importance are manuscripts in Gothic, Armenian, Georgian, Ethiopic, and Slavonic. Scholars study evidence preserved in all of these languages, for any amount of evidence is considered important. Supporting evidence is often found in these versions.

Quotations. Writings of many of the early "church fathers" have survived. These are studied for evidences for the early text of the New Testament. These writings include sermons and commentaries. There are enough of these quotations so that from them the text of the New Testament could almost be reconstructed. The most valuable quotations are those made in Syriac, Latin, and Coptic; but in preparing a printed Greek Testament today, over two hundred "fathers" are consulted. It is of great importance that the time and place of the writers is known. Quotations of the New Testament appearing in these writings show how certain passages read at these times and places.

Quotations of the New Testament found in early Christian writings cannot be used uncritically, for early Christians were not careful in citing the Scriptures. Writers like Origen (early third century) seldom quoted a passage the same way twice. They often quoted from memory. Sometimes they gave a paraphrase rather than an exact quotation.

Lectionaries. Worship was central in the life of early Christians, and the Scriptures were given a prominent place in church services. "Liturgy" was a means of involving the congregation in the service

---

[1] Cf. M. M. Parvis, "New Testament Text" *The Interpreter's Dictionary of the Bible*, IV, 594 ff.

of worship. They would join in the recitation of passages of Scripture. Passages from different parts of the Bible were sometimes brought together around one theme. Most of the lectionaries which have come down to us are late; even so, their evidence is not neglected.

Some Major Manuscripts

It would take far more space than is available here to describe all the manuscripts of the New Testament, but a closer look will be given to some of the most valuable ones.

Papyrus 52. This is a small fragment of a manuscript, only 2½ by 3½ inches. It contains only a few verses from John's Gospel (18:31-33,37-38). Its importance, however, is far greater than its size would seem to imply. It is the oldest copy of any part of the New Testament yet discovered. It was found in Egypt, and is now in the Rylands Library of the University of Manchester, England. The manuscript was copied probably about A.D. 130, within a generation of the writing of John's Gospel. The part of a leaf that survives is from a codex, that is, a book form, not a scroll. It is in Greek, written with pen and ink on papyrus. It proves that Christian Scriptures were used in codex or book form at least as early as the first half of the second century. It also shows that the Gospel of John was written early enough to have reached a town on the Nile River in the second century.

The Chester Beatty Biblical Papyri. An outstanding collection of papyrus manuscripts bears the name of Mr. Chester Beatty of London. In 1930-31 he acquired some ancient manuscripts in Greek which had been found in the sands of Egypt. The exact circumstances of the discovery are not known. Those who found them either did not know their value or were shrewd enough to know that by breaking them up they could get more money for them. Consequently, the original find is now distributed in several countries—some in Ann Arbor, Michigan, most of it in Dublin, Ireland, and some in Europe.

Papyrus 45 of Mr. Beatty's collection had 30 leaves of a papyrus codex which originally consisted of about 220 leaves, containing the four Gospels and Acts. The manuscript is from the third century and preserves a very early type of Greek text. Papyrus 46 originally consisted of 104 leaves, 86 of which remain. It contains ten letters in this order: Romans, Hebrews, 1 and 2 Corinthians, Ephesians, Galatians, Philippians, Colossians, and 1 and 2 Thessalonians. It seems not to have contained 1 and 2 Timothy or Titus. The manuscript was produced in the first half of the third century. It is the most valuable manuscript of Paul's writings known today. Papyrus 47 consists of ten leaves from the book of Revelation. The manuscript is from the third century. Few ancient manuscripts of Revelation are known, so this discovery was very important.

The Bodmer Library. Until 1956 the name Bodmer meant nothing to New Testament textual criticism. Now the Bodmer collection at Geneva, Switzerland, includes the most important discoveries of New Testament manuscripts since the purchase of the Chester Beatty papyri.[2] Both collections resulted from discoveries in Egypt. Although the Bodmer Library possesses early manuscripts other than New Testament ones, attention here is focused on four great New Testament manuscripts: Papyri 66, 72, 74, and 75. All are in the Greek language, written on papyrus, and in codex or book form. All have come to light since 1956.

Papyrus 66 was published in 1956, having been recently acquired by M. Martin Bodmer. The full story of its discovery in Egypt and how it eventually reached Switzerland has never been told. Economic and legal factors as well as personal and national interests were involved. Whatever that story may be, the manuscript is now in Cologny, a suburb of Geneva. It is a major source for New Testament textual criticism. The manuscript was produced about A.D. 200 and is thus one of the oldest known New Testament manuscripts. Papyrus 66 contains the Gospel of John, originally complete but now fragmented. The first fourteen chapters are almost intact, consisting of 104 pages. The remaining portion of the manuscript has survived only in fragments of forty-six pages. Enough of the text remains to be valuable in the effort to reconstruct the early text of John's Gospel. For example, the definite article in John 7:52 gives more point to the reading, "Search and you will see that *the* prophet does not rise from Galilee."

Papyrus 72 is a third- or fourth-century Greek papyrus codex containing a wide range of writings. Included are the Nativity of Mary, apocryphal correspondence of Paul to the Corinthians, the eleventh Ode of Solomon, the Epistle of Jude, a Sermon on the Passover by Melito of Sardis, a fragment of a hymn, the apology of Phileas, Psalms

---

[2] Cf. Bruce M. Metzger. *The Text of the New Testament* (New York: Oxford University Press. 1964). p. 39.

33 and 34, and 1 and 2 Peter.[3] At the University of Mississippi is the Crosby Codex, a Coptic papyrus manuscript probably from the third century, containing some of these same writings, all in some way related to the Passion and Resurrection. Both Papyrus 72 and the Crosby Codex came from Egypt.

Papyrus 74 is a seventh-century manuscript, originally containing 264 large pages measuring about 13 by 8 inches. It has been badly damaged, not strange for papyrus because of its fragile nature. It contains portions of Acts, James, 1 and 2 Peter, 1, 2, and 3 John, and Jude.

Papyrus 75 is an amazing manuscript. It contains most of the Gospel of Luke and much of John, 102 of the original 144 pages. It dates from around A.D. 200, estimates ranging from A.D. 175 to 225. Its text is very close to that of Codex Vaticanus (see below). It is more important even than Papyrus 66. The discovery of Papyrus 66 was almost too good to be true, and now we have Papyrus 75! Who knows what may yet come from the sands of Egypt or elsewhere? Papyrus 75 is the oldest known copy of Luke and one of the oldest of John. Less than a decade ago it was unknown. It is valuable throughout for the recovery of the text of Luke and John. Among its interesting readings are the ones in Luke 16:19, where the rich man is named "Neve," presumably "Nineveh," and in John 10:7, where Jesus is called "the shepherd of the sheep" rather than "the door of the sheep."

Codex Sinaiticus. The oldest complete New Testament known to us is called Codex Sinaiticus, because it was at Mt. Sinai until a century ago. Its "discovery" and "recovery" is a true story almost stranger than fiction. Except for the alertness of a young German scholar, Constantine Tischendorf, it probably would have gone up in smoke, being used to start fires in the Monastery of St. Catherine at Mt. Sinai. Fortunately, it was recognized for its worth and was preserved. It is a fourth-century Greek manuscript written in majuscule or uncial letters, codex in form, and written on vellum. It originally contained the entire Bible plus other Jewish and Christian writings (ten Jewish apocryphal books in Old Testament and the Epistle of Barnabas and the Shepherd of Hermas at the end of the New). It is now in the British Museum, London.

In 1844, Tischendorf visited the Monastery of St. Catherine as a part of an extensive search for biblical manuscripts. On the eve of

---

[3] Metzger, *op. cit.*, pp. 40 f.

his scheduled departure, he saw a wastebasket full of parchment (vellum) leaves and learned that two such baskets of discarded leaves had already been burned. He recovered from the basket 43 leaves which proved to be from the Greek version of the Old Testament known as the Septuagint (see below). His excitement was such that the monks, now sensing the value of the manuscript, refused to let him see the codex from which the leaves had come. On a second visit, in 1853, he saw nothing of the codex. On a third visit, in 1859, he presented the steward of the monastery with an edition of the Septuagint which he had just edited. The steward responded by showing Tischendorf a copy of the Septuagint which he had. It was the codex from which the leaves in the wastebasket had come!

Tischendorf managed to conceal his excitement and got permission to take the manuscript to his room for the night. It contained most of the Old Testament, all of the New Testament, plus the Epistle of Barnabas and a large part of the Shepherd of Hermas. The latter two writings were apparently considered canonical by the Christians for whom Codex Sinaiticus was produced around A.D. 375. It is now known that the Barnabas of Acts did not write this letter. Most Christians came to the position that neither the Epistle of Barnabas nor the Shepherd of Hermas was canonical. Tischendorf, through many negotiations and possibly through unfulfilled promises to the monastery, finally got the monastery to give the old Bible to the Czar of Russia, Greek Orthodoxy being the religion of both the Czar and the monks. In 1933 the manuscript was purchased by the British Museum for 100,000 British pounds, equivalent to about a half-million dollars (depression dollars!).

Codex Alexandrinus. This Greek manuscript was the first great acquisition of the British Museum and is sometimes referred to as the foundation of the museum. It dates from the early fifth century. In 1627 it was presented to King Charles I of England by Cyril Lucar, Patriarch of Constantinople. Like many of the oldest and best biblical manuscripts, it seems to have been produced in Egypt. In the fourteenth century it was returned to Egypt from Constantinople, and then in the seventeenth century it was returned to Constantinople.

When new, Codex Alexandrinus contained the complete Bible, several Jewish apocryphal books, treatises of Eusebius (d. 340) and Athanasius (d. 373), and 1 and 2 Clement. A late type of text is found in the Gospels, but the balance of the New Testament preserves an early type of text, like that at Alexandria, Egypt. It was the study of this manuscript which jolted those who had known only the text based on the work of Erasmus (that upon which English Bibles from Tyndale to the King James are based). Earlier and better manuscripts than Codex Alexandrinus are now known, but it played an important part in the quest for a better text. It is yet a serviceable manuscript.

Codex Vaticanus. The great fourth-century (about A.D. 350) manuscript known as Codex Vaticanus is often said to be the most valuable Bible known. No one can say what old manuscript is really the most valuable; some are invaluable, and that is true for Codex Vaticanus. It is older than Codex Sinaiticus and is more reliable, that is, it seems to be truer to the original text. It once contained the complete Old Testament, eight Jewish apocryphal writings, and the complete New Testament. It has suffered loss at three places: almost forty-six chapters of the beginning of Genesis, about thirty Psalms, from Hebrews 9:14 to the end of that epistle, 1 and 2 Timothy, Titus, Philemon, and Revelation. How and when this manuscript reached the Vatican Library in Rome is not known. Its presence there can be traced back to 1475, but how long it had been there at that time is unknown. For many generations scholars were denied access to it, but in 1889-90 it was made available in a complete photographic facsimile (each page photographed).

Codex Ephraemi. In the National Library in Paris is a fifth-century manuscript known as a palimpsest, a manuscript that has been scraped and used again. The manuscript was unbound and the sheets scraped during the twelfth century; and thirty-eight of the sermons of Ephraem, a Syrian of the fourth century, were written on some of the sheets. Of the Old Testament 64 leaves were used and of the New Testament, 145. Parts of every New Testament writing except 2 Thessalonians and 2 John are included in the 145 leaves used. Because ink penetrates deeply into vellum, some of it still shows underneath the newer writing. That is, much of the biblical text can still be read underneath the sermons of Ephraem. It is not surprising that it has been said that Ephraem's sermons were neither the first nor last to obscure the Bible. Of course, sermons can also open up the treasures of the Bible.

Codex Bezae. This codex illustrates yet another kind of manuscript. It is bilingual, written in Greek and Latin; Greek on the left and Latin on the right. The manuscript was written in the fifth century and was presented to Cambridge University in 1581. It is named for the reformer Theodore Beza, who gave it to Cambridge. It is the chief representative of what is known as the Western type text. The codex contains the Gospels and Acts. The Gospels appear in the Western order: Matthew, John, Luke, and Mark. The text preserved in this manuscript is very early and it differs widely from the type of text which was followed in Alexandria. In Acts, especially, the text is longer than that generally known. The most interesting reading is in the sixth chapter of Luke. Luke 6:5 appears after 6:10, and between verses four and five appear the words, "Man, if you know what you are doing, you are blessed; but if you do not know, you are accursed and a transgressor of the law."

It would be misleading to imply that these are the only New Testament manuscripts of importance. It would take volumes to describe all the great manuscripts in Greek and in early versions. These manuscripts may be seen in libraries and museums all over the world, some in the United States of America. Any good library has photographic facsimiles of some of the manuscripts, and most of them have been recorded on microfilm.

The Printed Greek New Testament

The student of Greek has a wide choice of printed Greek New Testaments. This has not always been true. Until 1516 it was not possible to own such a Greek Testament. The first Greek Testament to be both printed and published was that of Erasmus in 1516. A polyglot Bible (multiple languages) had been prepared in 1514 by Cardinal Ximines, but it was not until 1522 that it was released. Although its workmanship was superior to that of Erasmus, it has not directly contributed to the English Bible.

Erasmus. A Dutch scholar and humanist named Desiderius Erasmus prepared the text for the first printed Greek New Testament to be published. He dedicated it to Leo X, the Pope who withheld from Cardinal Ximines permission to publish his polyglot Bible until 1522. Apparently Pope Leo X had given Froben exclusive rights to publish the Greek New Testament for a limited period. Erasmus prepared a Greek text at the invitation of Johann Froben, a printer in Basle, Switzerland. Erasmus worked hastily and with only a handful of late manuscripts. This writer has held in his hands at one time all but one of the manuscripts used by Erasmus in preparing his text. Erasmus depended chiefly on two twelfth-century manuscripts. There was not a Greek copy of the book of Revelation in Basle, so Erasmus had to send for one. Reuchlin of Germany brought him a copy of Revelation, but it lacked the last six verses. Erasmus translated these verses from the Latin Vulgate into Greek. This Greek Testament went through minor revisions and was the basis for all English New Testaments from Tyndale (1525) to the King James (1611).

Westcott and Hort. Two great Cambridge scholars, B. F. Westcott and F. J. A. Hort, published in 1881 one of the greatest of all editions of the Greek New Testament. It utilized a wealth of source material and carefully tested principles of textual criticism. It had been 365 years since the first printed Greek Testament, and it was no easy step from Erasmus to Westcott and Hort. Many scholars had labored during the interval not only for knowledge but also for the freedom to utilize the knowledge they had. Memories are short, and the origin of the Greek text which underlay all English versions from Tyndale to the King James Version was soon forgotten if not deliberately ignored. Churchmen fought bitterly to retain the Erasmean text, resisting all new evidence and knowledge. It was not until 1831 that a great scholar, Karl Lachmann, dared to issue a Greek New Testament based upon the best manuscripts known and not limited to the "Received Text" based on Erasmus. Many other scholars labored before and after Lachmann, and many printed Greek Testaments were issued. The text of Westcott and Hort represented the best evidence, knowledge, and methodology of the day.

The Nestle text. In 1898 an eclectic text was issued by Eberhard Nestle, based upon the consensus of the Greek New Testaments edited by Tischendorf (1872), Westcott and Hort (1881), and Weymouth (1886, also a resultant text). This text, edited later by his son Erwin Nestle and now by Kurt Aland, has reached 25 editions. It is a highly serviceable and widely used text. Its recent editions are far more scientific than earlier ones, being based upon the latest knowledge of the text.

The Greek New Testament (1966). The most recent Greek New Testament is one published jointly by five Bible societies: The American Bible Society, British and Foreign Bible Society, National Bible Society of Scotland, Netherlands Bible Society, and Württemberg Bible Society. It bears the title, *The Greek New Testament.* This edition represents the very best of New Testament scholarship today. Behind the work of these Bible societies are the labors of countless men through many centuries: those who wrote under the inspiration of the Spirit of God, the scribes who did the tedious work of copying the manuscripts, scholars who sought out and studied the manuscripts, those who labored to work out principles for finding the best attested reading, where manuscripts differed, those who mastered the many languages in which the Scriptures appear, and not least, those who suffered reproach or even death for their labors in the interest of recovering the text nearest that of the original.

The New Testament Canon

The New Testament consists of twenty-seven writings: Gospels, Acts, Epistles, and Apocalypse. We are so accustomed to having it easily available in one bound volume that it is difficult to imagine Christians without it. It is hard to realize that Stephen never saw a copy of the New Testament. Paul wrote a considerable part of the New Testament, but in all likelihood he never even saw his own letters in one bound volume. Luke wrote the largest single portion of the New Testament (Gospel and Acts), but he never saw a complete New Testament. In fact, we have no evidence of all twenty-seven books in one bound volume until the fourth century. There may have been such a complete New Testament under one cover before this, but we have no evidence of it.

The New Testament books probably were written from about A.D. 51 or 52 until the last decade of the first century, about a half century in all. Recognition of some came early and for some only after a long period of testing and usage. The New Testament canon was largely settled by A.D. 200, but not until the fourth century was there anything like general agreement for the whole New Testament. Never has the whole Christian world been united on what books belong to the Old or New Testament.

The word "canon" is a Semitic word which has come to us through the Greek. It first was used for a cane or reed; then, it was used for a straight rod, hence a ruler, standard, or model. Used with reference to the Scriptures, it designates the writings accepted as unique and authoritative, books to be read and followed in synagogue or church.

The letters of Paul were probably the first books of the New Testament to be written. They were written over a period of little more than ten years, beginning about A.D. 51 or 52. It is not known when, where, by whom Paul's letters were collected and reproduced as one corpus (body of writings). The oldest manuscript of Paul's writings is Papyrus 46, dating shortly after A.D. 200. However, Paul's letters were known as a collection far earlier than that. Possibly the earliest reference to Paul's letters is in 2 Peter 3:16, where they were said to be hard to understand! Clement of Rome (ca. 96) and Ignatius (ca. 115) seem to have had some knowledge of Paul's letters. Possibly his letters had been collected by A.D. 90. Except for 1 and 2 Timothy and Titus, his letters were not contested in the early formation of the canon. Much of the Christian world did not judge Hebrews to be Paul's. It was not until the fourth century that it was generally accepted. It was accepted early in Egypt, as is reflected by its inclusion in Papyrus 46. In Rome and in the West it was thought not to be from Paul and was not accepted until the fourth century.

The Gospels and Acts were written probably from about A.D. 65 (Mark) until about A.D. 90 (John), with Matthew and Luke-Acts between Mark and John. The earliest known mention of a written Gospel is in the Didache (ca. 110, a book of teachings for a time thought to be by the apostles). From the early second century on, there are allusions to and quotations from the Gospels. By about A.D. 170 Tatian had woven the four Gospels into one unified book, the Diatessaron. By about A.D. 185, Irenaeus was arguing for the "quarternity" of the Gospels—that there could be only four, no more or no less. The oldest collection of the four Gospels and Acts is Papyrus 45, from the early third century. Papyrus 75, containing Luke and John, dates from possibly as early as A.D. 175. Marcion accepted only the Gospel of Luke. There were Gnostic groups which accepted other Gospels. But most of the Christian world seems to have received with little struggle the four Gospels belonging to our canon.

Beyond the Gospels, Acts, and the letters of Paul, the formation of the canon was not easy. There was no individual Christian or church council with the authority to settle the question of what writings were to be recognized as Scripture. Some writings were temporarily accepted, only to be rejected later when more was known about their origin. Some writings were rejected for a time and then generally accepted. The Christians of the world had to feel their way slowly along the difficult road which led to the New Testament canon.

There sere several basic criteria or tests by which Christians were guided as they sifted the many writings out of which emerged the New Testament. Apostolicity was a major test. They sought out those books which came from apostles, like Matthew, John, James, Peter, and Paul, or from men who had been associated with apostles, like Mark and Luke. Christianity is rooted in history, in an event. It is bound up with things done and said. Its origin is in Jesus Christ, one who lived in history. For this reason, the witness of the apostles was primary. These were men who had seen and heard Jesus and whom he had appointed to a special ministry of bearing witness to him. The New Testament is basically the apostolic witness.

Another test for Scripture was orthodoxy. The threat of heresy was one factor which drove the Church to formulate its canon. Marcion (*ca.* 150) rejected the Old Testament outright, holding that its God was evil and not the God of Jesus. He accepted only a short form of Luke (his Gospel) and ten of Paul's letters (his Apostle). A third test was universality, whether addressed to the whole church. This was not pressed, for some writings were addressed to individuals or local churches. The age of a writing and its usage were additional tests for canonicity.

Among the books temporarily accepted were the Didache (early second century), the Epistle of Barnabas (early second century), First Clement (*ca.* 95), Second Clement (*ca.* 150), and the Shepherd of Hermas (*ca.* 150). To a lesser extent books like the Apocalypse of Peter and the Acts of Paul, both obviously pseudonymous, were accepted in some circles. Clement of Alexandria (*ca.* 200) seems to have quoted the Didache as Scripture. The Epistle of Barnabas and the Shepherd of Hermas are included in Codex Sinaiticus (4th century). First and Second Clement are in Codex Alexandrinus (5th century).

The books most disputed before becoming generally accepted were Hebrews, 2 Peter, 2 and 3 John, Jude, James, and Revelation. Origen is the first writer known to have referred to the Epistle of James. Hebrews was accepted in Alexandria but rejected in Rome and in the West until late in the fourth century. Much of the Syrian church has never recognized more than twenty-two books, excluding 2 and 3 John, 2 Peter, Jude, and Revelation. The Ethiopic church added eight books to the canon generally accepted as New Testament. The Gothic church never accepted Revelation.

The earliest known list of New Testament writings corresponding exactly to our twenty-seven, no more and no less, appeared in the Easter letter of Athanasius, bishop of Egypt, in A.D. 367. By this time much of the church had come to agreement about which writings were canonical. It was in the fourth century that Christianity was freed from Roman persecution, the Emperor Constantine having been converted to Christianity in A.D. 314. With new freedom and new resources, and even active encouragement from the Emperor, Christianity moved into a new era of expansion and unity. It was in this period that the first great codices appeared, vellum manuscripts containing the complete Bible. All of these factors played some part in the finalizing of the canon. We may believe that through these many forces and factors and through human instrumentality the higher power of God's Spirit was at work, and by God's grace the New Testament has come down to us.

10.
Sources in Biblical Writings
Frank Stagg

Biblical writings may be seen from two perspectives: (1) from the viewpoint that they were given by inspiration of God and (2) from the viewpoint that they were given through human writers. There is no necessary conflict between these two views. In truth, the meaningfulness of the Bible is immensely enhanced by the fact that it is not only God's gift to man but God's gift through man. It was written by men, real human beings who were borne along by the Spirit of God and who spoke from God (2 Pet. 1:21). The Bible bears the marks of God upon it, and it also bears the marks of men. This is its glory and strength.

The Bible does not claim for itself the kind of origin claimed for the Koran (the sacred scripture of Islam) or for the Book of Mormon. The claim is made that the original text of the Koran is in heaven, inscribed on a great tablet beside the throne of Allah (40:3; 55:77; 85:22) and that it was sent down to Muhammad through the angel Gabriel or the "Spirit," sometimes called the Holy Spirit (26:193; 16:104). The theory is embarrassed by the fact that Muhammad revoked or abrogated certain verses of the Koran (2:100; 16:103 f.), an awkward theory if the original text is in heaven.[1] It seems actually that after Muhammad's death the "revelations" which had been given to him were for the first time brought together by Zayd, his secretary, and these later developed many variant readings, posing a problem that could be solved only by the substitution of a standard revised text to replace all the variant texts.[2] The Church of Jesus Christ of the Latter Day Saints (Mormon) claims that golden plates for the Book of Mormon were found under a rock in New York state. No

---

[1] Cf. *Encyclopedia Britannica*, 13:483 f.
[2] Cf. J. Christy Wilson, *Introducing Islam* (New York: Friendship Press, 1959), p. 27.

such claims are made for the Bible, and it is well that this is so. If the Word of God is to be understandable to man, it must be clothed in man's language. The Bible is the written Word, and it comes to us from God through human beings.

A parallel in some sense may be seen between Jesus and the Bible. The Word of God became flesh in Jesus Christ. He is both divine and human. His humanity is as real as is his deity. So it is with the Bible; it is God's Word coming to man "in the flesh." The analogy is not to be pressed too far, because the perfection found in Jesus is not found in other men. The Bible was given through living men, and their individual differences were not violated as the Word came through them. Through the centuries, the Bible has been copied by human scribes, translated from language to language by men, and interpreted by men. At every point may be seen upon it the marks of men but also the marks of God. The Bible belongs to the long and glorious story of God's dealing with flesh-and-blood men in revelation and redemption.

Seen thus, it is not surprising to find that biblical writers used sources in producing various books of the Bible. They wrote with pen and ink, and they wrote on parchment and on papyrus. In other respects, too, they utilized human resources in their writings. The experience, individual capabilities, and environment of each writer entered into the finished product. Luke's style is easily distinguishable from that of John. Paul's personality shines through every letter which he wrote. God used living men without blunting their individuality. Sources, too, written and oral, entered into the equipment of these men of old who "being borne along by the Holy Spirit, spoke from God" (2 Pet. 1:21, author's translation).

Luke's Statement About His Method

Of all the biblical writers, Luke comes nearest to telling us how he prepared for his task. His two volumes, Luke-Acts, begin with a preface:

Inasmuch as many have undertaken to draw up a narrative concerning the things accomplished among us, just as those who from the beginning were eyewitnesses and servants of the word delivered to us, it seemed good to me also, having traced out all things accurately from the beginning, to write to you in an orderly manner, excellent Theophilus, in order that you might know the certainty concerning the things which you were taught (Luke 1:1-4, author's translation).

In this preface he tells us much about his method and purpose. He recognizes the work of many others who already had drawn up narratives of the things accomplished among them. He does not specify any of these previous works, but in all likelihood the Gospel of Mark was one of them. He does not explicitly commend or disparage the works. Obviously, he saw something more to be done, else it would have been pointless for him to write another narrative. But he seems also to have been encouraged by the value of the previous works. He would build upon them and go beyond them, but he gives no hint that his purpose is to refute them. These works, or some of them, probably served as source materials with which he worked.

Luke indicates that he not only knew of earlier written works but that he consulted persons who had been eyewitnesses to events which he would narrate. It would have been pointless to mention eyewitnesses were their testimonies not utilized. Luke does not hesitate to allude to human resources upon which he drew. This is significant when one observes that no writer makes more of the Holy Spirit than does Luke. Inspiration and human agency are not irreconcilable; rather they are compatible. There is much truth in the old adage that God helps those who help themselves. After all, man's intelligence, his other gifts, and the world about him are provisions made by the same God who gives his Spirit without measure. When the Spirit of God inspires men, he does not override or negate their personalities, but heightens them. From Luke, as well as from other biblical writers, we may see that inspiration and human effort go together. This was true in the writing of the Bible.

The Synoptic Gospels

Comparative study of the Gospels of Matthew, Mark, and Luke discloses both striking similarities and differences. It is this combination of likeness and unlikeness which is referred to as the "synoptic problem." [3] In 1774, J. J. Griesbach published a synopsis of Matthew, Mark, and Luke (with some passages from John), and from this synopsis these three Gospels came to be known as the Synoptic Gospels. Griesbach shocked his readers by declaring that he would not "harmonize" much of the material in these three Gospels.

G. E. Lessing in a work published in 1784 (written in 1778) saw

---

[3] Synoptic is a Greek word used by scholars to refer to the basic outlook which is common to Matthew, Mark, and Luke. In a sense they "see together."

that the similarities and differences among the Synoptic Gospels required a theory of literary relationship, and he offered one. He theorized that there was an early Gospel, now lost, written shortly after the death of Jesus and known to the church Fathers as the Gospel of the Hebrews or the Gospel of the Nazarenes. It was written in Aramaic, the everyday, spoken language in Palestine in the time of Jesus. He further theorized that this Aramaic Gospel was translated into Greek by Matthew and by others and that these Greek versions of the earlier Aramaic Gospel stand behind our canonical Gospels. Thus, he saw that each canonical Gospel was based upon some Greek form of the Original Nazarene Gospel, resulting in basic authenticity with both similarities and dissimilarities.[4]

Lessing's theories have not stood up in the judgment of New Testament scholars, but the problems which he sought to solve have continued to challenge the scholars. How are the Synoptic Gospels related to one another? Did all three draw upon a common source, or did one influence the other two? The theory most widely held for more than a century is that Mark was probably followed by Matthew and Luke and that the latter two Gospels had other sources besides Mark.

The famous "four document" hypothesis is the theory that Matthew and Luke both followed Mark and another source called "Q," and that each had an additional source not used by the other, called "M" (source peculiar to Matthew) and "L" (source peculiar to Luke). It is best not to use the term "document" for Q, M, and L. These may represent specific written sources, but this cannot be proven. One is on surer ground if he recognizes basic categories or blocks of material in Matthew and Luke. The letter "Q" stands for the German word *Quelle*, meaning spring or source.[5] This material, common to Matthew and Luke but not to Mark, is known as the Logia. This may point to one written source, but this can only be a deduction from a comparative study of Matthew and Luke. There is a block of material common to Matthew and Luke but not in Mark, and it possibly came from one written source, but it could have been made up of more than one source, written and oral.

[4] Cf. W. R. Farmer, *The Synoptic Gospels* (New York: The Macmillan Co., 1964), pp. 3-6.
[5] Actually it is not known for certain how or when "Q" was first used as a symbol for sources. That it stands for *Quelle* is best attested theory. Cf. Stephen Neill, *The Interpretation of the New Testament*, 1861-1961 (New York: Oxford University Press, 1964), p. 119.

"M" stands for material found only in Matthew, and "L" stands for material found only in Luke. Again, all that can be said with certainty is that each of these Gospels has some material not found elsewhere. Mark has almost no material not found also in Matthew or Luke or both. Thus four great blocks of material may be distinguished: Mark, "Q," "M," and "L." Behind these blocks of material may have been various written and oral sources. To some of these Luke may have referred in his Preface (1:1-4). The following diagram illustrates this particular source theory:

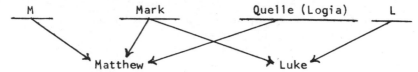

Much debated are the theories of Ur-Marcus, Proto-Luke, and Proto-Acts. *Ur* is a prefix from the Greek meaning "original, primitive." *Proto* is from the Greek meaning "first." According to some scholars, there was an early form of Mark used by Matthew which accounts for some of the differences between our present Mark and Matthew.[6] B. H. Streeter (1924) and Vincent Taylor (1926) argued strongly for a Proto-Luke. This is an early form of Luke consisting of L plus Q and our present Luke resulting from a later reworking of Proto-Luke in combination with Mark.[7] In this theory L + Q = Proto-Luke, and Proto-Luke + Mark = Luke. A Proto-Acts theory has been proposed recently, although the idea is not new.[8] All of these theories have been argued cogently by able scholars, but no conclusive case has as yet been made for any one of them. All such theories reflect the complexity of the Gospels and leave open the question of sources and stages of development. "Assured results" are hard to come by and hard to retain.

Priority of Mark

Until far into the nineteenth century it was believed that the Gospel

[6] For discussion of theory Ur-Marcus, see F. C. Burkitt. *Gospel History and Its Transmission* (Edinburgh: T. & T. Clark, 1907), pp. 40-58; and Pierson Parker. *The Gospel Before Mark* (Greenwich, Connecticut: The Seabury Press, 1953).

[7] B. H. Streeter, *The Four Gospels* (5th impression; New York: St. Martin's Press, 1964), pp. 199-222; and Vincent Taylor, *Behind the Third Gospel* (Oxford: The Clarendon Press, 1926).

[8] Cf. A. Q. Morton and G. H. C. MacGregor. *The Structure of Luke and Acts* (New York: Harper and Row, 1964).

of Matthew was earlier than that of Mark. Early Christians seem
not to have given much attention to Mark, seeing Mark as an abridg-
ment of Matthew. Papias (*ca.* 140) referred to Mark as the "interpreter
of Peter"; and later in the second century Mark was called the
"stump-fingered," either because he had small fingers or because of
the brevity of his Gospel (Anti-Marcionite Prologue, *ca.* 160-180).
Clement of Alexandria (*ca.* 200) held that the Gospels with genealogies, that is, Matthew and Luke, were written before those without
genealogies, that is, Mark and John (Eusebius, *Eccl. Hist.*, Vi. 14.5).
Augustine claimed that the order of the Gospels was Matthew, Mark,
Luke and John and that each wrote with a knowledge of his predeces-
sor or predecessors.[9]

Until the nineteenth century, Mark's Gospel was the most neglected
of the four, but since the mid-nineteenth century it has been considered
the earliest of the four Gospels and the basis for Matthew and Luke.
In 1832 Frederick Schleiermacher advanced the theory that Papias
knew a Gospel written by Mark (but not our Mark) and a collection
of sayings of Jesus (Logia) drawn up by Matthew.[10] Schleiermacher
did not go so far as to view these two works as the sources behind
the canonical Gospels. He followed Griesbach in believing that Mark
was dependent upon both Matthew and Luke. He thought that
Matthew drew upon the Logia (sayings of Jesus, later denoted by
"Q"), Luke upon Matthew, and Mark upon Matthew and Luke.[11]

In 1835 Karl Lachmann, in a comparative study of the Synoptics,
saw that when the order of materials varied in these Gospels either
Matthew or Luke was supported by Mark. This suggested to him
that Mark in some form was the Gospel being followed.[12] He saw
Matthew as based upon an Ur-Gospel and the Logia known to Papias.
He saw this Ur-Gospel to be best preserved in our Mark. It remained
for F. Weisse to go the next step in seeing Matthew as dependent
upon Mark (canonical Mark seen as identical with the Mark known
to Papias) and the Logia, both thought to belong to the eyewitness
period. This is what is known as the "two-document hypothesis."[13]
Weisse himself later abandoned the theory, holding that Matthew,

[9] Farmer, *op. cit.*, pp. 1 f.
[10] Cited by J. M. Creed. *The Gospel According to St. Luke* (London: The Macmillan Co.. 1930). p. XLVI.
[11] Farmer, *op. cit.*, pp. 8, 15.
[12] Creed. *op. cit.*, pp. XLVII f.
[13] Farmer. *op. cit.*, pp. 22.f.

Mark, and Luke were all dependent upon an Ur-Marcus. It was under H. J. Holtzmann (1863) that the two-document hypothesis triumphed, for Weisse himself had made few if any converts until Holtzmann accepted the theory as proven. It soon was generally accepted that Mark and a second source, eventually called "Q," lay behind Matthew and Luke.

As early as 1892, A. T. Robertson suggested to John A. Broadus that he prepare "a harmony of the Gospels which would depart from the old plan of following the feasts as the turning points in the life of Jesus." [14] Robertson's *Harmony* continues that of Broadus (1893), with Mark in the first column and the other Gospels arranged in the order of Mark, as far as possible. Robertson's *Harmony of the Gospels* (1922) and all books based upon it assume that Matthew and Luke used Mark as a source. In 1924, B. H. Streeter in *The Four Gospels* developed the strongest case yet for the four-document hypothesis. [15] Although some scholars challenge the theory of "Q" and some reject the theory that Mark was used by Matthew and Luke, [16] these seem to remain the best working hypotheses for synoptic study.

Of the 661 verses in Mark, the subject matter of only 65 is absent from Matthew; and only 31 verses of Mark appear in neither Matthew nor Luke. [17] This is strong evidence that Mark was used by Matthew and Luke. The theory is also reasonable, for it is understandable that Mark would be expanded by Matthew and Luke, but not that Matthew or Luke would be reduced to Mark. Those who hold that Mark was written after Matthew or Luke can offer no convincing explanation as to the need Mark would meet for readers who already possessed either of the fuller Gospels.

Form Criticism

About the beginning of the twentieth century, scholars began a new line of investigation of the materials behind Old Testament writings. By the end of World War I the method had been extended to the study of the Gospels and became known as "form criticism." This is an effort to get behind the earliest written sources and recover

[14] A. T. Robertson, *A Harmony of the Gospels for Students of the Life of Christ* (New York: Harper and Brothers, 1922), p. vii.

[15] Streeter, *op. cit.*, pp. 149-360.

[16] Cf. B. C. Butler, *The Originality of St. Matthew* (Cambridge: The University Press, 1951); and Farmer, *op. cit.*,

[17] Cf. C. S. C. Williams, "The Synoptic Problem," *Peake's Commentary on the Bible*, p. 748.

the earliest oral form in which biblical tradition [18] was formed or transmitted.

A basic presupposition in form criticism is that folk memory operates with small units, that is, that ordinary people remember and relate things that happened and things said in small units. In repeating these happenings and sayings they tend to follow certain literary forms.[19] The tradition of any group of people takes its earliest shape in the everyday life of the people. It is assumed that the tradition which found its way into biblical writings went through a period of oral formation and transmission before it was written down.

It is inconceivable that people around Jesus did not in his own time talk about him and about his deeds and words. Thus the "tradition" began before the crucifixion of Jesus. After his death and resurrection, his followers would repeat things said by Jesus and repeat stories of what he had done. As they gathered in homes night after night, it would be natural for one to say, "Do you remember?" or "I remember that day when. . . ." Those who had seen and heard Jesus would want to share their memories. Newcomers would want to know what he was like. Besides this, there would be problems and needs of various kinds to arise in the Christian community. These needs and questions would be met by the telling of some deed or by the recalling of some word from Jesus. Thus the tradition took shape. Jesus was remembered; the memories were interpreted, and they were preserved and applied.[20]

Various settings or life-situations probably formed the background or provided the occasion for the shaping of some of the material which eventually entered into the making of the New Testament. Early Christians gleaned from the Old Testament various passages which to them were testimonies (testamonia) to Jesus. These Old Testament testamonia would serve both to clarify their own understanding of Jesus and to defend their faith as they interacted with Judaism. Preaching and teaching needs formed the occasions for further gathering and shaping of materials. Worship needs would lead to the shaping of some of the material into hymns. Thus, narratives, sayings, hymns, confessions, and other units of gospel tradition took

---

[18] Tradition here is used as in 2 Thessalonians 2:15; 3:6; simply to designate what is transmitted and not to question its validity.

[19] Cf. K. Grobel, "Form Criticism," *The Interpreter's Dictionary of the Bible*, II, 320 f.

[20] Cf. John Knox, *Jesus, Lord and Christ* (Reissued; Harper and Row, 1958) for a study of this theme.

shape and were transmitted orally for a time and then were written down in more substantial sources.

Although form criticism has often yielded negative results, it need not do this. On the positive side, it stresses the importance of the community in the formation of the tradition and in its preservation. Between what was said and done, and the incorporation of this in biblical writings, may be an unbroken line of transmission: witnesses, those who first recited the events or sayings, the gradual formation of the oral tradition, the written sources, and finally the biblical book.

Sources in Acts

Many scholars are of the judgment that sources were employed in the writing of the book of Acts. There is much disagreement as to the identity and number of sources employed. If sources were used in Acts, these sources have not survived. It is only by analyzing the text of Acts that one can detect possible sources.

The most widely-held theory of sources in Acts relates to the "we-sections," i.e., the sections of Acts written in the first person (16:10-17; 20:5-15; 21:1-18; 27:1 to 28:16; and also 11:28 in the Western text).[21] Some scholars hold that the author followed a travel diary for these sections, possibly his own. Others hold that at most he may have had a few notes for this section.[22] The early chapters of Acts seem to reflect an Aramaic background, but it is not clear whether or not there were Aramaic writer sources behind these chapters.[23]

One of the most recent attempts to distinguish sources in biblical writings is one which employs the electronic computer, marshalling statistics about the occurrence of words, length of paragraphs, etc.[24] Morton and MacGregor argue for a Proto-Acts that began with 1:12-14; 3:1-10; and 4:1 to 5:12a; with 1:1-11; 1:15 to 2:47; 3:11-26; and 5:12b-42 added later from a secondary source.[25] The computer is highly serviceable for anything that lends itself to statistical measurement.

[21] Cf. Jacques Dupont. *The Sources of Acts*, tr. by Kathleen Pond (London: Darton. Longman and Todd, 1964), p. 52, who traces theories regarding the "we" sections in Acts to B. L. Konigsmann (1798); and *Ibid*, p. 33, the theory of parallel sources in Acts to F. Spitta (1891). A. Harnack. *The Acts of the Apostles*, tr. by J. R. Wilkinson (New York: G. P. Putnam's Sons. 1909), ch. 5 *et passim*, built upon Spitta's theory, arguing for two recensions for the early part of Acts.
[22] Cf. A. Harnack, *Luke the Physician*, tr. by J. R. Wilkinson (New York: G. P. Putnam's Sons, 1907), p. 53.
[23] Cf. Matthew Black. *An Aramaic Approach to the Gospels and Acts* (2nd ed.; Oxford: Clarendon Press. 1954).
[24] This has been attempted in Acts by Morton and MacGregor. *op. cit.*
[25] *Ibid.*, pp. 36, 44.

But in any writings there are personal factors which doubtless elude the machine, however efficient it might be otherwise. On the other hand, the computer may detect evidences which offer support to source theories arrived at by other means. It is doubtful that Morton and MacGregor are correct in their theory of Acts, although the probability of sources behind Acts is not to be excluded. The computer may prove to be important for source criticism in the years ahead, but as yet it is of limited value.

Hymns, Confessions, Liturgy

There are what seem to be traces of old hymns, confessional statements, or liturgical elements in many biblical writings. The New Testament clearly quotes the Old Testament many times, and it may also embody some early Christian prayers, hymns, or other formulations. For example, Ephesians 5:14 may preserve part of an early Christian hymn: "Arise, one sleeping, and stand up out of the dead ones, and the Christ will shine upon you." A stanza of an early Christian hymn about the Christ seems to appear in 1 Timothy 3:16 (author's translation).

He was manifested in the flesh,
He was justified by the Spirit,
He was seen by angels,
He was preached among the nations,
He was trusted in the world,
He was received up in glory.

An early confession or hymn may be reflected in 2 Timothy 2:11-13 (author's translation).

If we suffer together, we shall live together,
If we endure, we shall reign together,
If we deny (him), that one will remain faithful,
If we are faithless, that one will remain faithful,
For he is not able to deny himself.

Such examples could be multiplied. The Gospels of Luke and John, the epistle to the Hebrews, the Revelation, and other New Testament writings contain much that may have been taken over from the faith and worship of the early Christians.

The Old Testament

It is well known that many controversies have raged over the question of sources behind the first five books of the Old Testament, that is, the Pentateuch. Strangely enough, many who accept the theory of sources behind the Gospels find such theories offensive when applied to the Pentateuch. Whatever be the case with the Pentateuch, at least it should be recognized that if sources could be used in the writing of one biblical book, they could be used in another. Of course, the appearance of sources in one writing does not necessarily mean that they were used in another.

It seems that three conclusions may be reached: (1) Sources have not been absolutely proven behind any biblical book, although their presence seems obvious in certain books, and their use seems to be affirmed by Luke. (2) If sources are recognized in one biblical writing, no new principle or problem is necessarily introduced in seeing them in other biblical writings. (3) The question of sources for any biblical writing is to be answered in terms of an examination of that book itself.

Source analysis of the Pentateuch is usually traced back to Jean Astruc, a French Catholic physician, who when nearly seventy years of age published a work entitled, *Conjectures on the Reminiscences Which Moses Appears to Have Used in Composing the Book of Genesis* (1753).[26] He was seeking explanation to three questions: (1) repeated narratives of the same event, (2) the appearances of two names for God, "Elohim" and "Jehovah," and (3) problems in chronology, He arranged the material in the Pentateuch in four parallel columns, representing what he thought to be four major sources. He further divided the fourth source into nine subsources.

The source theories of Astruc were reworked by many scholars, gaining their widest acceptance through the work of Reuss, Graf, Kuenen, and Wellhausen in the last quarter of the nineteenth century.[27] It was chiefly Julius Wellhausen of Tübingen who perfected the JEDP hypothesis, which was accepted by many as among the "assured results" of biblical study and severely denounced by others. (Wellhausen identified the four major sources by the symbols "J," "E," "D," and "P." "J" designated the source which used the name of Jehovah from the beginning. "E" was the prophetic source which used the name *Elohim* for God before God revealed his name to Moses. "D" was the deuteronomic source, characterized by the concept of the

[26] K. Grobel, "Biblical Criticism," *The Interpreter's Dictionary of the Bible*, I, 410.
[27] D. N. Freedman, "Pentateuch," *The Interpreter's Dictionary of the Bible*, III, 724.

holiness of God. "P" was the priestly source, marked by a formal style with frequent repetitive phrases.) Never has the issue of sources behind the Gospels been debated so heatedly as were the theories championed by Wellhausen. One would think that more resistance would have arisen to source theories with respect to the Gospels.

Many scholars today see several major sources behind various Old Testament writings, believing these Old Testament books to have been produced by stages. They see an underlying source, referred to as "G" (*Grundlage*, i.e., foundation or underlying source). They think that it goes back to the twelfth or eleventh century B.C. and that its contents are scattered through books from Genesis to Joshua.[28] In this approach "J" is traced back to the tenth or ninth century, "E" to the ninth or eighth century, "D" somewhat later, and "P" to the time of the Exile.[29]

Strong challenge to the theory of written sources, like JEPD, now comes from critical scholars themselves. For some, the emphasis has shifted from written to oral sources. Form-critical study of the Pentateuch was given a strong impetus by Hermann Gunkel (1902); and it, at least in some quarters, is now given greater emphasis than are the theories of written sources. The Scandinavian school (centered in Uppsala, Sweden) holds that oral tradition played a more important role in the formation of the Pentateuch and other Old Testament books than is generally recognized. It is held that although much of the technical and legal material now belonging to the Pentateuch was written down in early sources, the narrative traditions were transmitted orally.[30] Blocks of material are seen to have been gathered to meet worship needs and other needs of the people as they met under varying circumstances at different times and in different places. The same story may have been used in different localities and times, and applied in each case to the needs of a particular time and place. This may account for the presence of the same story more than once in the Pentateuch. It also suggests the legitimacy of adapting or applying a narrative or saying to particular situations today. With the help of archaeological findings, much progress has been made in reconstructing different life-situations in which biblical materials were shaped, in each case reflecting that life-situation and meeting

[28] Freedman, *op. cit.*, III, 714.
[29] *Ibid.*, pp. 714-717.
[30] *Ibid.*, pp. 725.

its needs.

Some scholars today contend that exponents of the literary-critical method, that is, those who make written sources primary, do not give adequate recognition to the place oral transmission held in the ancient world. These scholars hold that the spoken word was prized above the written word, and that ancient people gave more attention to memorizing than do moderns. Present-day contempt for "learning by heart" was not characteristic of ancient Semites.[31] The primary place given to oral tradition (the spoken word) is traceable to both the preference for the more personal, spoken word and to the willingness to commit a great body of material to memory. An amazing power of memory is credited to many ancient people. For example, Johanan ben Zakkai could recite the Mishna [32] by heart, and he knew how long it would take to recite each paragraph.[33] (The Mishna is divided into sixty-three tractates which are subdivided into chapters and paragraphs, a total of about 790 pages.) Modern dependence upon writing has resulted in less reliance upon memory.

It is possible that much of the material which came to be incorporated in the Old Testament lived for generations through oral transmission. It probably took shape at various shrines or centers of worship, as at Shechem, Shiloh, Bethel, Gilgal, and Jerusalem. Some of the traditions may have had simultaneous development in several centers. This may account for some of the duplications and variations within the Old Testament. Festivals and great events like an enthronement (cf. Ps. 95) may have occasioned some of the materials. Prophets like Jeremiah probably depended mainly on the spoken word, writing down their message when it became necessary for another to deliver it (cf. Jer. 32:12; 36:4).

But the shrines, sanctuaries, and festivals were not alone responsible for the transmission of these materials. In every devout home in Israel, the father taught the law to his household, especially to his sons (cf. Ex. 12:26; 13:8,14; Deut. 4:9 f.; 6:7,20 f.; etc.).[34]

Scholars today are suspicious of "assured results." Although they generally recognize that written and/or oral sources were probably

---

[31] Eduard Nielson, "Studies in Biblical Theology No. 11," *Oral Tradition,* Chicago: Alec R. Allenson, 1954), p. 19.

[32] The Mishna is the "Second Law" of the Jews, the basis of what became the vast Jewish Talmud.

[33] Nielson, *op. cit.,* pp. 20 f.

[34] *Ibid.,* p. 58.

employed in the writing of many biblical books, not only the Pentateuch and the Gospels, they see the theory in vogue as being at most the best working hypothesis thus far developed. Short of the recovery of an actual document, one can establish only probability, not certainty, for a written source. Oral sources are even more elusive. We have the Gospel of Mark, and it can be tested alongside Matthew and Luke. Of all source theories, the use of Mark by Matthew and Luke is most nearly proven. Even this theory continues to be challenged by a few able scholars. Theories about G, J, E, D, and P in the Pentateuch and Q, M, L, Ur-Marcus, Proto-Luke, Proto-Acts, etc., with respect to the New Testament have been cogently argued. They may be true but finality yet eludes the scholars. It is even harder to recover or reconstruct the situations which probably belonged to the periods of oral transmission.

If these theories are correct, they do affect one's understanding of date, authorship, and manner of composition for biblical books. The theories as such do not rule out a meaningful doctrine of inspiration. The fact of inspiration is independent of the method through which writings were produced by men who were "borne along by the Spirit of God." It is not to be overlooked that the Spirit of God could move those who gathered and shaped the early oral and written sources even as he inspired those through whom the biblical writings were brought to their final form. The Spirit of God is not limited to one time or to one method. The strength of the Bible does not rest upon the inspiration of only a few individuals but upon a living community stretching over several thousand years.

The trustworthiness of biblical writings may be enhanced, not lessened, by theories of oral and written sources. It may mean that the gap between the time of the events narrated and the time of writing is filled by many witnesses who gave their witness both through oral and written transmission. The question of sources is a valid one, whatever the evidences may imply. On the other hand, the questions of inspiration and authority are not settled by source theories alone. It is to be observed that some who are convinced of the employment of sources in both the Old and New Testaments are among those who read the Bible with devotion and are assured that it conveys to man the Word of God.

11.
The English Bible

Frank Stagg

The Bible which undoubtedly is best known and loved by English-speaking people is the one popularly known as "the King James Version." A look inside most editions of this version will disclose the fact that it says of itself, "The Holy Bible, containing the Old and New Testaments, translated out of the original tongues, and with the former translations diligently compared and revised by his majesty's special command. Appointed to be read in the churches." This version, published in A.D. 1611, was the third English version of the Bible to be authorized by the rulers of Britain to be read in the churches. But what about before 1611? When did the Bible first appear in English? How did it come about? When did the English language arise? Was there an English language in the time of Jesus? These are among the questions which any reader might ask as he holds a Bible in his hands.

Today there are many Bibles from which one may choose. The Bible has been translated into more than a thousand languages and dialects. Most of those who read these lines read English alone, so their personal needs must be met by the English Bible. Even in English, there are many choices. In any good book store today one may find various English translations or versions, made over a period of more than three and a half centuries, from the King James Version to translations made a very short while ago. In all likelihood other translations are being made while these lines are being written, if not by some committee at least by individuals.

One recent publication, *The Four Translation New Testament*, brings together four versions of the New Testament in one volume, The King James Version, The *New American Standard Bible*, C. B. Williams' *The New Testament in the Language of the People*, and W. F. Beck's *The New Testament in the Language of Today* (Moody Press, 1966). The four versions are printed in parallel columns, two per page on each opening. This is a highly serviceable combination.

Should the English reader want to select only one translation for study, possibly The *New American Standard Bible* or the Revised Standard Version would best serve his needs (but see end of this chapter). The former is the careful work done by a committee, first published in 1901 and reissued with minor changes in 1963. The latter was published in 1946 (N. T.) and 1952 (O.T.). *The New English Bible* (1961) is competent and has the advantage of freeing itself from older patterns, taking fuller advantage of new knowledge. The King James Version remains a cherished Bible, but it is the hardest to understand, in part because the English language has changed considerably since 1611. Discovery of many old manuscripts of the Bible and a better understanding of biblical language also contribute to the advantage of new translations.

At this point it may be best for us to go back and see the beginnings of the Bible in English, tracing the history of the English Bible to our day.

The English Language

There was a time when there was no English language. The Bible had been completed long before the English language arose. Jesus, John, and Paul lived at a time when the English language was yet to arise. The earliest traces of Old English or Anglo-Saxon writings are around A.D. 737. Most of the manuscripts containing Old English come from the ninth and tenth centuries. English grew out of the Western branch of the Germanic or Teutonic family. Germanic speech probably reached Britain during the fifth or sixth century through heathen invasions by the Angles, Saxons, and Jutes. The Old English which first developed is like a foreign language to English-speaking people today. Roman missionaries introduced many Latin words into the Old English. Scandinavian and other influences continued to modify the language.

The three major stages of development in the English language are usually called Old English, up to about A.D. 1100; Middle English, into the fifteenth century; and Modern English, to the present. The language is alive and constantly changing.

Three Periods of the English Bible

The three major periods in the history of the English Bible roughly parallel the stages of development in the English language.

(1) Translations from the Latin Vulgate.—This period began about A.D. 670 and reached its climax in 1382 when John Wycliffe completed the translation of the Latin Vulgate into English.

(2) Translations based upon the first printed Greek New Testament.—This period began when William Tyndale in 1525 translated the Greek New Testament into English.

(3) Translations based upon Greek texts carefully reconstructed from the oldest and most reliable sources available.—This period began in 1881 when the English Revised Version was translated from a Greek text based upon ancient sources.

The Earliest English Translations

The first Bible known to have been used in Britain was the Latin Vulgate (prepared by Jerome from about A.D. 383 to 405). Christianity seems to have reached Britain by the third century.

Bede, bishop of Jarrow, said that Caedmon (d. 680), an untutored man with a gift of song, turned parts of the Latin Bible into verses for song. The Old English into which he rendered the Latin is as foreign to us as Latin itself, if not more so. His work, as that of Cynewulf in the ninth century, was paraphrase, not strict translation.

The first person known to have made an actual translation of any part of the Bible into English was Aldhelm, bishop of Sherborne. About A.D. 709 he seems to have translated the Psalms into Old English. Bede made translations from the New Testament and, according to Cuthbert, was translating the Gospel of John when he died in 734. King Alfred the Great (871-901) had various religious books translated into English, and he translated a few passages from the Old and New Testaments.

Among the earliest extensive renderings of the Latin New Testament into English were interlinears added to Latin Gospels. The Lindisfarne Gospels were copied in Latin in the seventh century. In the tenth century Aldred, a priest, wrote between the lines a word-for-word translation into the Northumbrian dialect of Old English. The Wessex Gospels (from about the tenth century) are the oldest independent extant translations of the Gospels into English. Later in the century

Aelfric, Abbot of Enysham, translated parts of several books of the Old Testament.

After the Norman Conquest (1066) the English language underwent major changes. Traces of various translation efforts survive, but not until the fourteenth century was the whole Bible translated into English.

John Wycliffe and the English Bible

The first translation of the complete Bible into English was made under the influence of John Wycliffe (1328-1384). It is not clear whether Wycliffe did any of the translating, but at least he was the force behind it. Wycliffe taught at Balliol College, Oxford, and was rector at Lutterworth. England was divided between clerical and anti-clerical forces. Wycliffe was anti-clerical and had the support of John of Gaunt. Wycliffe held that the individual was directly answerable to God in terms of God's law as found in the Bible. For this reason, he held that the Bible should be translated into the language of the common man.

It seems that there were at least two Wycliffe versions of the Bible—an early one produced about 1380-1384 and a revision after his death in 1384. The early work may have been done by some of his students, particularly Nicolas of Hereford, and possibly his secretary, John Purvey. The revision made after Wycliffe's death is probably due to John Purvey. Both versions were made from the Latin Vulgate, including the Apocrypha in the Old Testament. The earlier version was almost a word-for-word rendering of the Latin. The later Wycliffite version was truer to the English idiom.

In 1382 an attack was made upon Wycliffe in a sermon preached at St. Mary's College, Oxford. Wycliffe's teachings were denounced as heretical, and he was forced to leave Oxford for Lutterworth, where he died eighteen months later. The clerical party condemned the Wycliffe Bible; nonetheless, it was widely read. Handwritten copies were limited and costly. A complete Wycliffe Bible sold for what would equal several hundred dollars today. Some farmers paid a load of hay for a few chapters of Paul or James. To possess and read the Wycliffe Bible was not only costly; it was dangerous.

In 1408 the Archbishop of Canterbury, Arundel, influenced the Provincial Council at Oxford to prohibit any translation made by a private person, aiming the ban at the Wycliffe Bible. It was under such circumstances that the complete Bible was first translated into and read in English. It was the scholar Wycliffe who insisted that the Bible be placed in the hands of the common man.

William Tyndale and the English Bible

A major epoch in the history of the English Bible is that ushered in by William Tyndale's translation of the New Testament from Greek into English in 1525. This era reached its climax in 1611 when the King James Version was published. English translations of the Bible before Tyndale had been made from manuscripts of the Latin Vulgate. Tyndale worked from a printed text of the Greek New Testament.

The invention or discovery of printing was one of the most significant events in modern history. Although the Chinese and Japanese had some form of printing centuries earlier, the art was independently discovered in Europe during the fifteenth century. Although disputed, the earlier printing in Europe is probably to be credited to Johann Gutenberg. It is customarily said that the Latin Vulgate was the first book to be printed, but there may have been earlier works. The famous Gutenberg Bible (Latin) was probably begun in 1449 or 1450 and completed in 1455.[1] About forty copies of this edition survive. Early printings of the Bible were no more accurate than the handwritten copies, but they were produced in far greater numbers than had been possible in manuscript.

The invention of printing in Europe coincided almost exactly with the introduction of the Greek Bible into Western Europe. When Constantinople fell in 1453, many Greek-speaking Christians found their way into Western Europe, taking with them the Greek New Testament. In the fourteenth century Wycliffe knew neither Hebrew nor Greek, but in the fifteenth century Christian scholars were attracted to both of these biblical languages. By the early sixteenth century the Greek New Testament was printed.

The first complete Greek New Testament to be printed was the Complutensian Polyglot, that is, a multilanguage Bible. The Old Testament was printed in parallel columns of Hebrew, Latin, and Greek. Someone who thought that the Latin Vulgate was the only true Bible said that placing it between the Hebrew and Greek was like crucifying Jesus between two thieves. The New Testament was

---

[1] Cf. M. H. Black, "The Printed Bible," *The Cambridge History of the Bible,* ed. by S. L. Greenslade (Cambridge: University Press, 1963), p. 415.

printed in two parallel columns of Greek and Latin. Although its six volumes were printed between 1514 and 1517, it was not published until 1522. Meanwhile, in 1516, a Greek New Testament was printed in Basel, Switzerland. The text was prepared by Erasmus for the printer Froben. This Greek text, with minor revisions, was the basis for the translation published by William Tyndale in 1525. The work of Tyndale was the foundation for the King James Version (1611), although a number of important versions intervened.

William Tyndale is one of the greatest names in the history of the English Bible. He was educated at Oxford (B.A., 1512; M.A., 1515), and then did further study at Cambridge, possibly studying Greek there. He became the tutor to a prominent British family and there debated the Scriptures with many churchmen who visited in the home. To one opponent he issued the challenge, "If God spare my lyfe, ere many yeares I wyl cause a boye, that dryveth the plough shall know more of the Scripture than thou doest." He seems to have echoed a statement made by Erasmus in his Greek New Testament. Erasmus had written in the preface of his Greek New Testament in 1516:

I totally disagree with those who are unwilling that the Holy Scriptures, translated into the common tongue, should be read by the unlearned . . . I could wish that even all women should read the Gospel and St. Paul's Epistles . . . I wish that the farm worker might sing parts of them at the plough, that the weaver might hum them at the shuttle, and that the traveler might beguile the weariness of the way by reciting them.[2]

In 1523, desiring to publish an English translation of the Greek New Testament, Tyndale sought the backing of Cuthbert Tunstall, bishop of London, but without success. He went to Germany and began to print his English New Testament at Cologne. The project was reported to city senate, and Tyndale was forced to flee to Worms with the sheets already printed. There he succeeded in having 6,000 copies printed, many of which reached England by April, 1526. Church authorities in England tried to destroy all copies of Tyndale's work, burning the copies found. Tyndale twice revised his English New Testament, 1534 and 1535; and he began translation of the Hebrew Old Testament into English. It is his 1534 revision that proved to

[2] Cf. F. F. Bruce, *The English Bible* (New York: Oxford University Press, 1961), p. 29; and A. Wikgren, "The English Versions of the Bible," *Peake's Commentary on the Bible*, ed. by Matthew Black and H. H. Rowley (New York: Thomas Nelson and Sons, 1962), p. 25.

be the foundation to many later versions, including the King James.

Tyndale was opposed in part because he had violated a prohibition passed in 1408 in Oxford against private translation of the Scriptures. He was also opposed because of notes and prefaces in his edition which took up the Protestant cause, especially the Lutheran views.

Luther was opposed in England by the highest authorities. King Henry VIII in 1521 had published a work against Luther, *Assertion of the Seven Sacraments.* For his work King Henry had been hailed by Pope Leo X as "Defender of the Faith," a title yet borne by British sovereigns.[3] The fact that Luther in 1522 had translated Erasmus' Greek New Testament into German may have stimulated Tyndale to do the same in English. Tyndale could not afford outwardly to identify with Luther, but he shared many of Luther's views.

In 1531 Tyndale pledged that if Henry VIII would grant him the freedom to publish the bare text of the Scriptures he would write nothing more. Despite his pledge, however, his work was not licensed in England. He took refuge in the free city of Antwerp. In May, 1535, he was kidnapped and imprisoned in a dungeon outside Antwerp. After months of suffering, he was brought out of the dungeon, strangled and burned on October 6, 1536. His dying prayer was, "Lord, open the King of England's eyes!"

From Tyndale to the King James Version

The Coverdale Bible (1535). Martyrdom ended Tyndale's effort to translate the complete Bible into English, but the work was continued by one of his associates, Miles Coverdale (1488-1569). On October 4, 1535, Coverdale's complete English Bible was published. Coverdale lacked Tyndale's skill in biblical languages and did not translate directly from Hebrew and Greek. He relied upon various authorities in Latin, German, and English in composing his work. Tyndale's work was one of his sources; but because of the feeling against Tyndale, he made no explicit reference to him.

Coverdale was educated in Cambridge and was an Augustinian friar until he left the order under influence of the Protestant Reformation. Several times he moved back and forth between England and the Continent, governed by the attitude of the reigning monarch toward the Reformation. Coverdale not only published what is known

---

[3] Bruce, *op. cit.,* pp. 29 f.

as the Coverdale Bible (1535), but he edited the Great Bible (1539) and had some part in preparing the Geneva Bible (1560). The 1535 edition was the *first complete Bible to be printed in English* (Wycliffe's complete English Bible was handwritten, not printed until 1850). It was also the first English Bible to separate the Apocrypha from the Old Testament books and print them as an appendix.

Coverdale's Bible was never formally authorized by the King of England, but Henry VIII did give oral sanction to it in the presence of the bishops as he said, "If there be no heresies, then in God's name let it go abroad among our people." The Coverdale Bible had been printed on the Continent but soon was sold in England. Copies sold in England contained a dedication to Henry VIII, and the new translation won the backing of Thomas Cromwell, powerful statesman. Thomas Cranmer, Archbishop of Canterbury, in 1534 led the bishops to urge the King to order the translation of the Bible into the common English tongue and that it be delivered to the people for their instruction. A bishops' Bible was not produced until 1560, and meanwhile Cranmer supported the reading of other English versions.

The Thomas Matthew Bible (1537). The English Bible known as Thomas Matthew's was no doubt prepared by John Rogers, associate to Tyndale. The pen name was used probably to avoid the stigma of association with Tyndale. When Tyndale was arrested in Antwerp, he turned over to John Rogers the work on the Old Testament. The Thomas Matthew Bible is more a revision of Tyndale than a new translation. Thomas Cranmer, Archbishop of Canterbury, was sufficiently pleased with Matthew's Bible to write Thomas Cromwell urging him to try to get Henry VIII to license this version to be sold and read until such time as the bishops put forth a better one. His pessimism about the production of a bishops' Bible is reflected in his closing remark, ". . . which I think will not be till a day after doomsday."

Henry VIII licensed Matthew's Bible as well as the 1537 revision of Coverdale's Bible. These were not formally "authorized" versions, but they were given royal license to be sold and read in England. Both depended heavily upon the work of Tyndale. Both circulated freely in England the year following Tyndale's death! Thus the first English Bible to be published with royal license was largely Tyndale's work.

Taverner's Bible (1539). The influence of Tyndale is seen in the

Taverner's Bible, a revision of Tyndale by Richard Taverner, a layman, a graduate of Oxford and skilled in Greek. His version was of great merit, but it was overshadowed by the Great Bible, which was published very shortly after Taverner's Bible.

The Great Bible (1539). The Great Bible gets its name from its size, the pages being 15 by 9 inches. No press in England could handle a page so large, so the work was sent to Paris for printing. It was Cromwell who initiated this version, encouraging Coverdale to prepare a new English Bible. Apparently there was opposition to the Matthew's Bible because it was basically Tyndale's work and it carried controversial notes. But the foes of Tyndale did not escape him in the Great Bible, for it was but a revision of Matthew's Bible, in turn based upon Tyndale's Bible. On the frontispiece of the Great Bible was a picture of King Henry VIII delivering the Word of God to Cromwell and Cranmer, who in turn delivered it to the clergy and laymen.

The second edition (1540) carried these words on the title page: "This is the Byble apoynted to the use of the churches." The second edition also carried a preface written by Archbishop Cranmer. Because of this it is sometimes called Cranmer's Bible. Later editions made even more explicit the royal backing of the Great Bible. The title page included the words, "auctoryed and apoynted by the commandmente of our moost redoubted Prynce and soveraygne Lorde Kynge Henry the VIII, supreme heade of this his churche and realme of Englande." By 1540 the new title page made reference to Cuthbert, Bishop of Durham. This is the Cuthbert Tunstall who, as bishop of London in 1523, had denied Tyndale the backing he sought. Thus another opponent of Tyndale's ended up supporting a version which was largely based upon the work of Tyndale.

The Geneva Bible (1557-1560). Persecution of Protestants was a factor in the production of the Geneva Bible, one of the better English Bibles. Roman Catholic reaction brought about the fall and execution of Thomas Cromwell in 1540 and forced Henry VIII to change his rather liberal policies. In 1543 he banned all translations bearing the name of Tyndale and ruled that no laboring man or woman be allowed to read the Bible. Eventually only the Great Bible was permitted, and it was limited to the upper classes.

Henry VIII was followed to the throne by his son Edward VI (1547-53). Edward was a Protestant and sought to restore the Bible to the people. In 1553 he was succeeded by Mary Tudor, a Roman

Catholic, who caused three hundred Reformers to be executed, including Cranmer and John Rogers. The 1538 order that the Great Bible be placed in the churches was not revoked, but many Bibles were burned.

Coverdale and many others took refuge in the free city of Geneva. Led by William Whittingham, a group of great scholars worked for two and a half years in producing what is known as the Geneva Bible (sometimes called the "Breeches Bible" because it followed Wycliffe in translating Genesis 3:7 so as to have Adam and Eve making breeches for themselves). It was the first English Bible to employ verse divisions. In the New Testament it followed those developed by Robert Estienne for his 1551 Greek New Testament. For the Old Testament it followed verse divisions from the Hebrew Bible.

The Geneva Bible was completed in 1560 and continued its influence long after the Bishops' Bible and the King James Version were published. It was the Bible of the Pilgrim fathers, John Bunyan, Shakespeare, and even King James. For fifty years it was the favorite Bible of the common people of England and Scotland.

The Bishops' Bible (1568). Although superior in quality, the Geneva Bible was not so popular in England as in Scotland, because it carried strongly Calvinistic notes. In 1561 Matthew Parker, Archbishop of Canterbury, proposed a revision of the Great Bible. The work was completed in seven years, the work being done by bishops and scholars who later became bishops. They avoided bitter and controversial annotations or notes. The translation represented a "safe" compromise for public reading. In effect it became the second "authorized" English Bible for the Church of England, the Great Bible being the first. It was based upon the Great Bible and was itself the basis for the King James Version.

The King James Version

Probably no English Bible will ever be so greatly loved by so many people as has been true for the King James Version of 1611. Many seem to forget that many English versions preceded it and that it was not so well loved in its earliest years. In fact, it was severely criticized by some and neglected by others in favor of older versions, especially the Geneva Bible. Some of the very bishops who produced it continued to use the Geneva Bible for their own sermons. The Puritans favored the Geneva Bible because it was Calvinistic in tendency. The King James Version had no theological annotations, but its language favored Anglican theology.

Strangely enough, it was from the Puritan side of the Church of England that the proposal for a new translation came. King James (who was James VI of Scotland before becoming James I of England when Elizabeth I died on March 24, 1603) called a conference of churchmen and theologians at Hampton Court in January, 1604. John Reynolds, a Puritan, proposed that a new translation of the Bible be prepared in place of "those which were allowed in the raignes of Henrie the eight, and Edward the sixt, were corrupt and not answerable to the truth of the Originall." His intention possibly was to express displeasure with the Coverdale Bible and the Bishops' Bible, possibly hoping for recognition of the Geneva Bible. King James was pleased with the suggestion for a new translation, expressing his judgment that the Geneva Bible was the worst of the translations. Most scholars consider it the best of the time.

Within a month, James had worked out careful plans for the new version. He appointed leading scholars from Oxford and Cambridge Universities and Westminster Abbey. Fifty-four men were selected, and it seems that at least forty-seven of them engaged in the work. They were divided into six groups to work in three companies: two at Westminster, two at Cambridge, and two at Oxford. To Westminster was assigned the work on Genesis through 2 Kings, and Romans through Jude; to Cambridge, 1 Chronicles through Ecclesiastes, and the Aprocrypha; and to Oxford, Isaiah through Malachi, and the Gospels, Acts, and Revelation.

Careful rules were drawn up for the project: (1) The Bishops' Bible was to be the basis for revision, changes to be made only as required by the underlying Hebrew and Greek texts. (2) Biblical names were to remain as near as possible to the forms already in use. (3) Old ecclesiastical words were to be retained, like "church" rather than "congregation." (4) Words with more than one usage were to be translated according to the requirements of context and "faith." (5) Chapter divisions were to follow those of the Bishops' Bible. (6) Marginal notes were not to be added, except as needed to explain Hebrew or Greek words. (7) Cross-references to relevant biblical passages were to be made. (8) Translations or revisions were to be made by individuals and then checked by the whole company. (9) Each company was to submit its completed work to the other two companies for their approval. (10) Where companies did not reach agreement, final decision was to be sought in a general meeting. (11) Help from any learned man in the country could be sought, (12) Each bishop was to help secure names of those "skilled in the tongues." (13) Company chairmen were to be the Deans of Westminster and Chester and the King's Professors of Hebrew and Greek at Oxford and Cambridge. (14) Readings from Tyndale, Matthew's Bible, Coverdale, the Great Bible, and the Geneva Bible were to be followed when they seemed truer to the text than those of the Bishops' Bible. (15) Three or four senior divines not otherwise engaged in the project were to supervise the implementation of rule four.[4]

The King James Version was carefully produced. It depended heavily upon the work of Tyndale and Coverdale. The revisers also made use of the Hebrew and Greek texts as well as Latin versions. The Greek text for the New Testament was based upon rather late manuscripts. Since the revision was done by the Church of England, it is not surprising that it favors Episcopal terminology.

The English of the King James Version is generally well suited to public reading. There are some rough renderings, as "Whom do men say that I am?" There were printing errors, most of which were removed. One printing error remains to this day and confuses the meaning of Matthew 23:24. "Strain *at* a gnat" should have been "strain *out* a gnat," i.e., filter out. Several minor revisions took place from 1629 until 1769. Although its preface affirms that it was "appointed to be read in the churches," there has never been a formal authorization of the "Authorized Version." For all practical purposes, it was the third English Bible to be authorized by civil and ecclesiastical authorities.

The Revised Version

Not until 270 years after the publication of the King James Version (1611) did another major one appear, the English Revised Version (New Testament, 1881, and Old Testament, 1885). A number of attempts at revision were made during the nearly three centuries between, but they were either abortive or of no lasting influence. This was in striking contrast to the production of at least eight major

[4] Cf. Grant, *op. cit.*, pp. 74 f.

versions from Tyndale (1525) to the King James (1611), only 86 years.[5] In a sense, the work from Tyndale to the King James was one continuing work, all based on substantially the same Hebrew and Greek texts and all dominated by the work of Tyndale.

The Revised Version (1881-1885) grew out of a proposal made in 1870 by the Province of Canterbury to the Province of York that together they appoint a committee to revise the Authorized Version of the New Testament. York declined but Canterbury went ahead, extending the revision to include the Old Testament. The first proposal was to limit the committee to Anglicans, but this was changed to include Nonconformists (others than the Church of England). Although mostly Episcopalian, the committee included Presbyterians, Baptists, Methodists, Congregationalists, and one Unitarian. Two companies were formed, one for each Testament. Both companies met at Westminster Abbey for their work.

An American Committee was formed to work with the English Committee. However, it was so late getting started and had such disagreements within the Committee that it did not share in the Revised Version, except through American preferences listed at the end of the English volume.

The Revised Version was hailed with much fanfare, two Chicago papers printing the New Testament text in Sunday supplements. This version never supplanted the King James, however. It was based upon a better Greek text for the New Testament, and scholars had better knowledge of Hebrew and Greek. The textual critics, B. F. Westcott and F. J. A. Hort, exercised great influence in the committee. But the revisers were too much bound to the past. Their English was more archaic than that of the King James. Translations in some places were so literal as to miss or obscure the meaning. Furthermore, major breakthroughs in the recovery of ancient biblical manuscripts and the study of New Testament Greek came after the issue of the Revised Version.

The American Standard Version

The American Standard Version (1901) is the American counterpart to the English Revised Version (1881-85). Bound by contract, the American Committee was not free to issue a revision until fourteen

[5] This does not include the Roman Catholic Bibles in English, the Rheims (1582) and Douai (1610) Versions of the New and Old Testaments or several somewhat isolated Protestant efforts.

years after the completion of the English Revised Version. The 1901 publication represents work done independently in America, although it had received its initial impulse from England. The version adheres closely to the Hebrew and Greek texts as then known. The English style does not have the charm of the King James Version and the renderings are sometimes pedantic. The updating of this version under the name *New American Standard Bible* (1963) gives it a new lease on life. Although generally competent, the American Standard Version in its old or new dress does not reflect the full competence of biblical scholarship.

The Continuing Task

Translations and revisions of the Bible continue to appear. Some twentieth-century productions represent committee work, and many are the translations of individuals. Among these are *The Twentieth Century New Testament* (1899-1901); translations by James Moffatt (1913-26), R. F. Weymouth (1903), E. J. Goodspeed (1923), Helen B. Montgomery (1924), J. B. Phillips (1947-   ), C. B. Williams (1937); the Revised Standard Version (1946-52), and *The New English Bible* (1961).

The Revised Standard Version (1946-52). Copyright to the American Standard Version (1901) was acquired in 1928 by the International Council of Religious Education, representing forty major denominations in the United States and Canada. In 1937 the Council authorized a revision of the American Standard Version. The revision was to be thoroughgoing, yet it was to remain within the tradition established by Tyndale. It was to be suited to public reading and also to religious education. It was to capture the simple, classic English style of the King James Version, yet utilize the best biblical knowledge available. The goals of the committee were met with reasonable success. Like all translations, it reflects human weaknesses and limitations. The violent controversies which it touched off in many places were often uninformed. Many of the renderings which were protested had been introduced years before in widely read versions. One publisher found itself in the awkward position of having published for years a reading (*parthenos* rendered "maiden") which it condemned in the Revised Standard Version. The RSV has "young woman" in Isaiah 7:14 but "virgin" in Matthew 1:23 and Luke 1:27.

The New English Bible (1961-   ). The proposal which led to the production of *The New English Bible* originated with the General Assembly of the Church of Scotland in 1946. The Church of England and the principal Free Churches in England were enlisted in the project. Leading scholars of Oxford and Cambridge were given responsibility for directing the work of translation. The Committee undertook to render the Bible in "timeless" English, to avoid archaisms and passing modernisms. They sought to be accurate without pedantry. They wanted the style to be suited to public, oral reading. This version has been well received to this point, and it is highly competent. It is a strange development that the King James tradition survives in the American-produced Revised Standard Version more so than in the British-produced New English Bible, for it is the latter which most nearly strikes out on a new path.

"Good News for Modern Man," The New Testament in **Today's English Version *(1966).*** This is a highly accurate and readable version. It is intended for the ordinary layman and meets that need. No translation is perfect or final, but this one should serve English-speaking people, scholars and laymen, for years to come. It is best used alongside some established version made by a recognized committee. Robert G. Bratcher, translator, is a scholar of first rank; and he had the advantage of working in the context of the American Bible Society. The inexpensiveness of this version places it within reach of any willing to read it. The Old Testament counterpart is under production by a number of scholars to whom the work is assigned.

The Jerusalem Bible (1966). This translation, under the editorship of Alexander Jones, is the work of translators who depended upon the pioneer work of the School of Biblical Studies in Jerusalem. It is based upon the original Hebrew and Greek. Published both with and without exegetical notes, it reflects the best of current biblical scholarship in both translation and notes. There are also introductions to the separate books of the Bible, abridged in the Standard edition. Beautiful maps and other helps are included. Remembering the human limitations upon all our work, this is a highly serviceable translation.

The New American Bible (1970). This is a translation by members of the Catholic Biblical Association of America, and it carries the imprimatur of the Archbishop of Washington, D.C. It reflects the new openness of the Roman Catholic Church to the Bible. This is an excellent translation, with a minimum of confessional bias, probably none deliberately so. It is made directly from the Hebrew, Aramaic, and Greek. Although basically the work of American Catholic scholars, begun twenty-five years ago, its committee was expanded following the Second Vatican Council to include non-Catholics. About fifty scholars produced the work. It includes the Old Testament Apocryphal books recognized in the Catholic Church. It explicitly acknowledges that a "perfect" work can be only a goal and not an achievement, but it does strive to be faithful to the intention of Scripture. This is among the competent translations of the Bible into English.

The Living Bible (1971). This possibly is the worst rendering of the Bible ever made into English. The author and publisher has only a superficial acquaintance with Hebrew and Greek. What he offers are his loose paraphrases made from an English text, not translations from the original languages. Along with loose paraphrases are actual mistranslations and distortions, traceable apparently to both ignorance and bias. The vulgarity introduced into 1 Samuel 20:30, crude as it is, is less serious than the obscuring or perverting of biblical intention here and there.

The New International Bible: New Testament (1973). This is an excellent work, produced by a committee both transdenominational and international. The final responsibility for this work was delegated to fifteen scholars, the Committee on Bible Translation, composed for the most part of biblical specialists from universities, colleges, and theological seminaries. Specialists in various fields, including English diction, were consulted. This is a highly competent work, rendered in readable, idiomatic English. Like other honest versions, it acknowledges human limitations and that all translations fall short of their aims. This version, within these limits, may be used with confidence and profit.

12.
The Book to Live By
Ralph A. Herring

From the sacred writings of other religions and those of the Christian faith, this chapter draws attention to the Bible as a book to live by. What is the Bible's place of authority in the life of the believer? The answer will be sought against the background of authority in general and in relation always to the authority of Christ and to that of the individual himself, for each person is an authority in his own right.

It would be difficult to overstate man's capacity for authority and the urgency of his need of it. Without authority society loses its cohesive force and lawlessness abounds. Riot runs amuck in the realm of human values. Examples of this tragedy are plentiful in all areas of life. But nowhere is the lack of authority more pathetic than when the void occurs within the person himself. Psychologists have a name for such a state. They call it *anomie* (pronounced án.o.mē, from a Greek word meaning "lawless"). According to Webster *anomie* describes a condition in an individual commonly characterized by personal disorientation, anxiety, and social isolation.

Through no choice of his own a babe is born into this exciting and terrifyingly complex world. Early in childhood he begins a restless search of his sourroundings to find out who is in charge. How far can he go in getting his own way? Where must he let another take over, and why? Each makes his own search. The quest for authority becomes actually, then, the quest for someone to give meaning and direction. It is the quest for a satisfying command, for the ennobling experience of accountability. It is the quest for backing, for the right of being, for one's authentication as a person. This quest extends to all levels and is basic to every relationship.

The Bible becomes actually a book to live by as one sees it within the framework of this complex and often painful process of seeking out and adjusting to authority. Questions arise in logical succession. What about man's capacity for authority? Granting that its nature is dynamic, where and how does the Bible fit into its flowing stream? In relationship to the written Word, how does one reconcile the ageless conflict between the letter that kills and the spirit that quickens? How may the believer find his own self-authentication?

Man's Capacity for Authority

The question of man's capacity for authority arises quite naturally at the beginning of this discussion. That capacity is his crowning dignity as a person. Every appeal of the Scriptures is made toward its development and direction.

There is, for instance, an illuminating passage from Proverbs: "He that is slow to anger is better than the mighty; and he that ruleth his spirit than he that taketh a city" (16:32). To rule is the act of a responsible being. It presupposes the capacity both to recognize and exercise authority. Man is to rule in the strategic realm of the spirit within him. All the lines of administration within the empire of his own being—soul and body—converge in the realm of the spirit. To rule there is his supreme challenge and his crowning achievement.

The great parable of Jesus on the wisdom of counting the cost reveals succinctly God's respect for the individual whom he confronts with the saving Word. "What king," asks Jesus, "as he goeth to encounter another king in war, will not sit down first and take counsel?" (Luke 14:31, ASV). Here is man the finite pitted against God the infinite, but king withal whether he sues for peace or perishes in folly.

The gospel of grace respects this kingly dignity of man by presenting God's bid for allegiance on the basis of individual acceptance. He makes man individually the unit for the administration of divine authority in all corporate relationships of which he is part. By the very nature of his Christian experience this is preeminently true in the church (1 Cor. 12:27). It is also true in the basic relationships of the natural order: the family, the tribe, and the state. Sometimes we speak of the Christian home or of a Christian nation, but the unit of measurement in such cases is the quality of Christians who are in such relations, the extent to which each for himself acknowledges and enjoys the authority of his Lord.

To consider the individual thus as a unit in corporate authority does not mean, of course, that the Christian significance of that relationship is arrived at by majority vote. The Bible plainly teaches the power of Christ's minority. The doctrine of a remnant by God's own selection and preservation is evident early in Scripture and is developed more particularly by Isaiah and Paul.

Conscience is another factor which should be considered as evidence of man's capacity for authority. But its great significance in this respect is often overlooked. It is generally thought that man rules by a balance of power achieved through the interplay of reason, emotion, and will. Thus, a metaphor attributed to Woodrow Wilson runs to the effect that reason reigns but does not govern. Man is governed rather by a tumultous House of Commons, his emotions, the prevailing one of which stands forth as prime minister to do his bidding. This is helpful. It came from one who went far in the process of government. But it should not be taken as a substitute for conscience.

According to the Bible conscience is an innate part of man's equipment, more complex and delicate than any electronic computer. Paul describes its function among people who had never heard of God's law. The voice of conscience is not always right, but neither is anything right which is done in violation of its integrity. However one may describe this inner voice which speaks in such imperial tones, its chief function seems to lie at the point of communication between man and the unseen. Though it is a part of man's natural equipment, it serves as a medium between him and the supernatural. Its purpose is to enable him to weigh his decisions in the context of eternity.

The function of conscience in this respect may be likened to that of a radio receiving set issued to a police officer. By it he hears the voice of his command. But this analogy would be instructive only if the underworld in his city were speaking on the same wave-length. The officer's response in that event could not be mechanical. It would necessarily be governed by his power of discernment in the light of all the truth available to him. He would then have to distinguish between the voices which came in over the speaker.

The Spirit of God brings conviction leading to decision through conscience. But this is not to say that the archdeceiver, as an angel of light, would not attempt to work his will through the same medium of communication. God and Satan speak to men on the question of the rightness and wrongness of their course. It is always possible, however, by an enlightened conscience to distinguish between what comes from God and what comes from Satan. Conscience, then, is the measure and guarantee of man's accountability. To it God makes his appeal, and so should we: "By manifestation of the truth commending ourselves to every man's conscience in the sight of God" (2 Cor. 4:2). Such is the approach by which the authority of God comes to grips with that of the individual.

The Flow of Authority

It has already been observed that authority is not static. It is a flowing thing. As with a stream of water or the current of electricity, there are channels or lines of communication. Always there is the power of motion. In tracing the flow of God's authority or power, special attention will be given to its source and effect because the nature of authority may be determined more readily by examining these than by examining the means or manner of its expression.

Its Source

The etymology of the word "authority" points like an arrow to the source. It is built upon "author," as the spelling indicates. It is a word of priority, of origin. The original is the authentic. The Greek word for authority is *exousia,* a compound of two words; one, a preposition meaning "from" or "out of"; the other, a participial form of the verb "to be." Milligan defines its meaning as "power of choice," "liberty of action"; and he refers to its "common usage in wills, contracts, and other legal documents to denote the 'claim,' or 'right,' or 'control' one has over anything." [1]

Moses' experience at the burning bush (Ex. 3:10-14) is an outstanding illustration of the importance of source to authority in the Hebrew mind. On that memorable occasion God revealed his name to Moses and commissioned him to deliver Israel from Egypt. Moses asked what he was to say to those who would inquire as to his authentication. God replied: "I AM THAT I AM. . . . Thus shalt thou say unto the children of Israel, I AM hath sent me unto you." The name Jehovah or *Ehyeh* or *Yaveh* is from the Hebrew verb "to be." In whatever language, ultimate authority derives from the One who eternally IS, the I AM.

[1] James Hope Moulton and George Milligan. *The Vocabulary of the Greek Testament.* (London: Hodder & Stoughton. 1930 ed.). p. 225.

The important question in the flow of authority is not *what* is said but *who* said it. Any man who has worn the uniform of his country will testify to this, and it is a good thing to remember when reading the Bible. The conflicts in authority which the Bible provokes are most readily resolved by tracing them faithfully to their source.

The story of Jesus in the home of Jairus is illuminating at this point. On the authority of their own information and instruction, the servants of Jairus came to him with the heartbreaking statement: "Thy daughter is dead: why troublest thou the Teacher any further?" (Mark 5:35, ASV). But when Jesus entered the home he said, "The child is not dead, but sleepeth" (v. 39, ASV). There seems to be flat contradiction between what Jesus said and what the servants said, and the effect is painful.

When the two statements are traced to their source, however, the conflict is resolved. Both are right. The servants and Jesus spoke from different levels of authority. He who could raise and restore the child to the family circle had every right to say she was but sleeping. Jairus did not deny the truth of what the servants said; he simply caught the overtones of a higher authority and placed himself under the command of the One who voiced it. By doing so he sets the student of the Scriptures a good example.

From its source the flow of authority actually starts with a word. John's opening statement in the prologue of his Gospel makes this clear: "In the beginning was the Word." The Genesis account of creation is in accord. There the record reads: "And God said, 'Let there be light'; and there was light" (Gen. 1:3, RSV). James links the Word of God in the closest possible sequence to his will. "Of his own will he brought us forth by the word of truth that we should be a kind of first fruits of his creatures" (James 1:18, RSV). The testimony of the centurion whose faith won the praise of Jesus illustrates and confirms the point in this paragraph. Schooled in the discipline of the Roman army, he knew that the flow of authority started with a word. "But say the word," he entreated, "and my servant shall be healed" (Luke 7:7, ASV).

Its Communication

In the communication of authority the valid place of the Scriptures themselves has already been described. No book of antiquity rests on better documentary evidence.

But there is another aspect to the communication of authority that deserves special note. Authority must not be confused with the impressive trappings which often attend it. The rating of persons who pass it on and the manner in which they do so are of secondary importance. A colonel's command is none the less to be obeyed whether it be given in the full regalia of his office or in fatigues, or for that matter, whether it be delivered by a corporal or a captain. The important thing is that the command be understood and obeyed forthrightly, unequivocally. The prophet Elisha's word to Naaman, the leper, was effective even though the proud general in the Syrian army was at first offended by its lack of pomp and circumstance.

This distinction is important because much that has been written in the Scriptures remains as anonymous as the hero of John 9. Anonymity, however, does not impede the flow of authority, nor does it detract from the splendor of heroism. The name of a prophet or a writer is not the important thing. Neither is his cultural background or social habit. These may differ as widely as those of Isaiah from those of John the Baptist. The tendency is to make too much of the prophet and too little of what he says. This exactly reverses God's order. If the words of Jesus are taken at the expense of what is said in the rest of the New Testament, the red letter editions will become a snare to those who read them. The important thing is that God's message gets through. "*All* scripture is inspired by God and is useful for teaching the faith and correcting error, for re-setting the direction of a man's life and training him in good living. The *Scriptures* are the comprehensive equipment of the man of God, and fit him fully for all branches of his work" (2 Tim. 3:16-17, Phillips, italics mine).

Its Effect

In Jesus the authority of God found perfect human expression and it did so as that authority was conveyed through human instrumentality. Working in reverse direction from the famous prologue of Hebrews, one might say: God could not (have) spoken to us in his Son except as he had previously spoken in the prophets in divers manners (Heb. 1:1-2). The events which prepared the way for the incarnation of Jesus were human events worked out in history through men and women who responded in faith to the Word of God.

In no event is this more clearly seen than in the birth of Jesus. That birth was the fulfillment of the prophetic word beginning from

Genesis 3:15 and continuing to the announcement of Gabriel. Hearing Mary's question, "How shall this be?" the angel added: "No word from God shall be void of power" (Luke 1:37, ASV). Through her response of faith (v. 38) and the Holy Spirit's quickening power, Jesus was born. "The word became flesh" (John 1:14). His arrival on the human scene, the quality of his life, the nature of his death and resurrection are all authenticated by Scripture. The Man Jesus Christ is, therefore, both the fulfillment and the confirmation of Scripture. And this is the unique glory of the Bible. A book that reveals Jesus can be relied upon to reveal also the true meaning of life, its eternal destiny, and the means which will lead to its complete realization.

The authority of the Scriptures, therefore, is of a kind with that of Christ himself. And to appreciate its peculiar quality, one should consider it in relation to other kinds of authority which compete for man's allegiance. One such claim is the right of priority. "I was here first," it says. Thus in the old days homesteaders and miners staked their claims; today inventors secure their patents. There is also the authority derived from force, where "might makes right." The nations of the world tremble under threat of a world holocaust if might should again become the ultimate court of appeal. Another form of authority rests on prestige or excellence by whatever means it may be achieved. To gain knowledge is to gain power. Especially is this true in an age which all but worships science. There are elements both natural and right in all these claims, but none of them speaks in the tone of life's supreme imperative.

That which is best in them all is gathered up in Christ. The hallmark of his authority is to be seen in its basis of appeal: whether to fear, which drives; or to love, which draws. On every occasion when the authority of Jesus was challenged, he cited to his critics God's redemptive love as his right for being and doing. Jesus staked his claim to lordship in the human heart upon that which he had done for man through the cross and the empty tomb.

The striking picture of the Messiah-King with which Matthew concluded his Gospel may well conclude this section also. He presented the crucified and risen Christ as the authority of God incarnate. In his portrait one sees Jesus gathering the reins of government into his nail-pierced hands. In supreme command of life and death his voice rings out: "All authority hath been given unto me in heaven and on earth" (Matt. 28:18, ASV). Caesars before and since have made their claims, but never man such as a claim as this one, validated now by his living presence. In Christ, God's authority rests fully and securely within the life stream of the human race, and because it does the Book which speaks of him and from him is securely there too.

The Letter and the Spirit

The object of concern in this section may be stated in the form of a query: In making the Bible a book to live by, how is one to chart a course between the letter and the spirit? Both are necessary; neither can give meaning and life without the other. But to be drawn to an extreme in either direction is fatal. The answer is that Jesus walked with perfect poise the narrow path between these extremes and the legacy of his Spirit provides that those who obey him may do so too.

Christ made this provision in three important transferrals which followed closely upon his victory over death and his dramatic claim to supreme authority. The first transference was from his visible presence among his disciples to his invisible presence in them through the Holy Spirit. The next was from his role as Messiah-King of the Jews to his role as Head of the Church, his body of believers redeemed from all races. Historically both of these transferrals were sealed on the day of Pentecost.

Less conspicuously and across the interval of time during which his apostles ministered to his followers, Christ transferred the written expression of his authority from the Old Testament to the New. This is not to say that the claims of the Old Testament Scriptures were no longer valid. But it is to say that certain features of Christ's role as Messiah depicted in the Old Testament were deferred in their application to the world scene, and that all of the old covenant must be understood and applied in the light of the new.

The point to emphasize in the transferrals is that after Pentecost there was an inwardness both as to the Scripture and the Spirit unknown before. This was new, but it was precisely that toward which the old covenant had pointed. Through the prophet Jeremiah God had distinctly said, "I will make a new covenant . . . I will put my law in their inward parts, and in their heart will I write it; and I will be their God, and they shall be my people" (Jer. 31:31,33, ASV).

Out of his trials as an apostle, Paul bore testimony to the fulfillment of this promise as an accomplished fact. More importantly for the purpose of this study, he also explained something of the way in which it came about. Writing to the church at Corinth he said, "Ye are an epistle of Christ, ministered by us, written not with ink, but with the Spirit of the living God; not in tables of stone, but in tables that are hearts of flesh . . . for the letter killeth, but the spirit giveth life" (2 Cor. 3:3,6, ASV).

In a remarkable way the passage just quoted reveals the complex nature of authority. It speaks of the authority of the Spirit, and of the living God, and of Christ, and of Scripture, and of believers themselves in a new covenant where their corporate relationship becomes an authentic "epistle of Christ." These different elements may be described in Dr. Bernard Ramm's apt metaphor as a "mosaic of authority." When they are related to the Bible in terms of sequence, its authority will be more readily appreciated.

On this basis attention is given first to authority within the Godhead. In this holy mystery God the Father initiates authority, God the Son mediates it, and God the Spirit administers it. The function of each is distinct but the effect is one. Some of the notes of a piano have three strings which blend in harmonious unity to enrich the overtones of the same wave length. Thus, in an infinitely higher realm, the triune God speaks through the Bible. The objective in the Bible is revelation: of God himself as Creator-Father to the reader, and of the reader to himself as created or begotten in his likeness. The Son is the medium of this revelation. He became man in order to communicate its fullness to men. The Spirit is the agent by whose inspiration the content of this divine revelation was penned upon the pages of Scripture.

It is evident from the foregoing that the Bible occupies an intermediate and unique position in the communication of authority from God to man. Like Christ himself, the Scriptures have both divine and human elements. This is necessarily so because if God is to be understood he must speak the language of men. Admittedly, there are difficulties in communication, the chief of which is finding that delicate balance between the letter and the spirit.

As Paul uses these terms in 2 Corinthians 3, "letter" and "spirit" are symbolic. Around each there is a cluster of ideas. The letter represents the objective, form, circumstance; the spirit represents the subjective, content, the essence of personal values. Spirit may be spelled with a capital "S" (Spirit of God, RSV) or it may be spelled with a small "s" (ASV). It refers to God's Spirit undoubtedly. But man's spirit and spirit in a general sense cannot be excluded. The authority of the Bible, thus, finds its way to the conscience of man *in the tension between the letter and the spirit.* It is through this illuminating combination that the "word of Christ" (Rom. 10:17) speaks in living tones and that the individual comes into his highest dignity as a person, competent and accountable for his own free response.

Players of musical instruments and singers *a cappella* often use a tuning fork to assure perfect harmony. The rigid prongs from which the tuning fork gets its name are made of steel. Neither prong of itself is capable of yielding a satisfactory pitch. But the vibration between the two of them establishes a wave length which will remain true to pitch as long as it can be heard. Such a tone at 442 wave lengths per second is called standard pitch, the authentic note for musicians all over the world. One may draw a helpful analogy by letting one prong of the fork represent the "letter" and the other, the "spirit." The stroke of circumstance on either prong sets going a vibration between them. In this manner one with a discerning ear may detect the authentic wave length of the Spirit's voice and respond in sympathetic vibration to the harmony of God's redemptive purpose. "He that hath an ear, let him hear what the Spirit saith unto the churches" (Rev. 2:7, ASV).

The Key to the Authentic Life

The decision to make the Bible a book to live by is not so easy or so simple as it may sound. It usually comes about after painful heart searching. Conflict naturally arises upon the confrontation between the authority of the Bible and that of the individual. There is one who sees to that and capitalizes upon it. He posed the issue to the first mother in Eden: "Yea, hath God said?" (Gen. 3:1). That this question was put at all is evidence that the great Parliamentarian of the universe ruled it in order. Every man must answer for himself.

There are steps familiar to all who have faced that question and answered it through the obedience of faith. First, one comes to realize that he is not sufficient as an authority in himself. Life is too complex. Though he may not know that Jeremiah stated his case so aptly, he concludes with the prophet, "I know that the way of man is not in himself: it is not in man that walketh to direct his steps" (Jer.

10:23). This conviction represents a long step forward. But there are other steps. To what or to whom shall he turn for direction? How shall he cull the best from the wisdom of the ages, or evaluate the findings of science? How shall he come by a satisfactory criterion of values?

The same desperation which forced one to look outside himself for an answer forces him now to turn from the wisdom of this world about him and to look upward. Thence God gives answer, not in a formula but in a mystery, in Christ. "In him is the yea"—life's affirmation; in him also is the amen—life's confirmation (2 Cor. 1:20). But the Christ of the answer is also the Christ of the Scriptures. Implicit in faith's surrender to the authority of Christ, therefore, is faith's surrender to the Bible's authority. The two are one and inseparable.

But the time comes when that which has been implicit must become explicit in a total commitment. The commitment may not be any formal confession as when a man receives Jesus as Lord and Savior, but it is definite and complete nonetheless. Results will make it evident. Here is the way one man expressed it.

"When I began to preach a few years ago," wrote the famed evangelist, Dr. Billy Graham, "I had many questions and some doubts about this Book. Intellectually, I could not figure it all out. Do you know what I did? One day in 1949 I opened up my Bible and I said, 'O God, I do not understand everything in this book. There are problems I cannot figure out. But, O God, from this day on I am going to accept this book by faith as the authority of my life and ministry.'

"My ministry changed overnight," he continued. "I found that I carried a sword in my hand. And I attest with Job, 'I have esteemed the words of his mouth more than my necessary food' (Job 23:12)." Billy Graham had made the Bible a book to live by.

But the greatest statement about the relation of faith to authority was not made by an evangelist, nor even a theologian. It was made by a layman, an officer in the Roman army of occupation during the days when Jesus was on earth. His experience sums up the important and practical application of the central truth in this chapter.

Teachers and philosophers are inclined to regard truth in terms of intellect, as something to be known. Theologians tend to think of truth in terms of doctrine and dogma, as something to be stated. But this centurion spoke of truth in terms of authority as something to be obeyed. Anything short of that was unthinkable to this soldier.

To him the power of Christ was of a nature similar to that which he exercised as an officer in the army, only upon an infinitely higher level. "But only say the word," he urged, "and my servant shall be healed." And there was the way he had it figured, "For I also am a man under authority, having under myself soldiers: and I say to this one, Go, and he goeth; and to another, Come, and he cometh; and to my servant, Do this, and he doeth it." The secret is the word "under." By accepting his place *under* authority he was *in* authority. As long as he stayed in line of command, all the authority of Imperial Rome was effective at his word. That is the way he explained it, and Jesus said he was right. He had found the key to an authentic life.

APPENDIX:
The World's Other "Bibles"
E. Luther Copeland

A few years ago a very large and useful volume was published
with the title *The Bible of the World.*[1] It contains selections from the
various sacred scriptures of the different religions. Actually, however,
the title is somewhat misleading. The world does not have one "Bible"
but many. Or, to put it more accurately, the world has many Bibles,
the different religions recognizing their own various scriptures.

There are several living religions today, all of which in some sense
have scriptures. These living religions are Christianity, Judaism,
Zoroastrianism, Islam, Hinduism, Buddhism, Jainism, Sikhism, Con-
fucianism, Taoism, and Shinto. The first four of these originated in
the Near East, the next four in India, and the last three in the Far
East. Most of these religions are ethnic faiths; that is, they are confined
to the national, cultural, or racial group of their origins. Only Christianity, Islam, and Buddhism—and to a lesser extent Judaism—have
spread beyond their original social group to the point of justifying
the term "world religion." Indeed, Christianity alone among the religions, from its beginnings until the present, has consistently made
a universalist claim and has believed itself to be destined, in some
form or other, to be the religion of the whole world.[2]

Characteristics of Religious Scriptures

In the various religions, what distinguishes "the scriptures" from
other literature? It is not necessarily their "religious" character. Much
religious literature is not considered "scripture" at all, and some
portions of the scriptures are not directly religious. Practically all kinds

[1] Robert O. Ballou. *The Bible of the World* (New York: Viking Press. 1939).
[2] See A. C. Bouquet. *The Christian Faith and Non-Christian Religions* (New York: Harper and
Brothers. 1958). pp. 1-3.

of literature are found within sacred scriptures: history, poetry, fables, proverbs, legal codes, myths, drama, prophecies, genealogies, etc. Certain passages taken out of their context would reveal no special sacredness, yet the whole has somehow come to be specially revered as sacred. What, then, are the characteristics of scriptures which set them apart from other literature? There are several distinguishing marks,[3] though some scriptures do not exhibit all of these characteristics.

In the first place, the sacred literature or scriptures of a religion are in some sense regarded as "inspired." That is, they convey a wisdom or knowledge which comes from the mystic or superhuman world. It is not quite correct to say that the scriptures of the various religions are considered to be the word of God or the gods, because some religions, for example, Jainism and early Buddhism, are atheistic. In their case a mystic knowledge derived from man's religious intuition is transmitted through the scriptures.

The quality of inspiration, therefore, varies with the different religions; so, also, does the degree of intensity of the inspiration. Moreover, the way inspiration is interpreted may vary widely among the adherents of a given religion, as we know from the different theories of inspiration among Christians. Likewise, the attitude toward inspiration may determine just how sacred or "sacrosanct" the scriptures are to be held. If one believes, for example, that the scriptures are divinely inspired in such way as to render them entirely unique and infallible, he is apt to resist any attempt to study them critically and scientifically. Such resistance is sometimes seen among adherents of various religions, including Christianity.

In the second place, since they are believed to be divinely inspired, the scriptures become the source of authority for a religion. In Christianity, we speak of the Scriptures as the authoritative rule of faith and practice. This same conviction is to be found among other religions concerning their own scriptures, though some religions are more "scriptural" than others. Of course, attitudes toward scripture vary widely within a given religion.

In the third place, the scriptures of a religion usually have official limits placed upon them. They are limited to a "canon." In the

Charles S. Braden. *The Scriptures of Mankind* (New York: The Macmillan Company. 1952). pp. 6-9.

development of a religion, a canon of scripture is usually decided upon relatively quickly—at least within a few centuries! To add books to this canon is prohibited, unless the religion is usually flexible; and to make such additions is to incur the charge of heresy.

In the fourth place, the diverse teachings of scripture are often summarized as creeds or confessions in order to focus the authority of scripture. The scriptures themselves may be too diffuse and diverse to function handily as a "rule of faith and practice." Creeds, then, bring scriptural authority into sharper focus, often setting forth authoritative teaching, or belief concerning contemporary issues confronting the religion.

Finally, in addition to creeds, there is often a body of related literature which supplements the canon. This "supplementary literature . . . while theoretically less sacred, does nevertheless constitute a highly important source of direction for faith and practice." [4] Many Christians regard very highly the "Church Fathers" of the early centuries of Christian development, while certain denominations prize the writings of their founders. In Islam the *Hadith* or "Traditions" are very important, and in Hinduism there is a distinction between scriptures of primary authority and secondary authority (*sruti* and *smriti*, respectively).

A Description of Some Non-Christian Scriptures

Since there is not space here for a treatment of the scriptures of all ten of the non-Christian religions mentioned previously, only those of three major religions—Hinduism, Buddhism, and Islam—have been chosen to illustrate the different types of sacred books and of attitudes toward them by those believing in their authority.

Scriptures of Hinduism

It is natural to turn to the scriptures of India first, for some of these are undoubtedly the most ancient scriptures of any religion—in point of oral composition if not of writing. No doubt Hinduism, the faith of about 85 percent of the nearly five hundred million people of India, is the oldest living religion. Its origins hark back to the second or third millennium before Christ.

Hinduism is not only the oldest but also the most diverse of the

---

[4] *Ibid.*, p. 8.

world's religions. It presents a baffling variety of religious beliefs and practices, as well as a bewildering vagueness. Hinduism has no founder and no definite creed. At heart, also, it recognizes no final or absolute revelation. It absorbs and includes all kinds of religious beliefs and expressions in India—if these will permit it—from the crude, primitive religion of hill tribes and the polytheism of peasants, to the lofty philosophy and not uncommon agnosticism of the intellectuals.

The scriptures of Hinduism, as one would expect, are likewise rich in diversity of types of literature and ideas. Composed over many centuries, the scriptures include hymns and prayers, meticulous instructions for ritual, regulations for life in society, profound philosophical discourses, and many other elements. The religious and philosophical ideas are not only diverse but often contradictory.

Yet in all this bewildering diversity there is a certain unity, a central core of common beliefs or presuppositions. Prominent among these are belief in *varnashrama*, the caste structure of society; *karma*, the moral law of cause and effect; and *samsara*, reincarnation or transmigration of souls. So far as the individual is concerned all that one is at present is determined by his karma, what he has done and been in an endless chain of previous lives. And what he shall be in future lives, whether in this world or some other, depends upon his karma, what he has been and done and what he now is and does. The central quest of Indian religion, therefore, to which the scriptures give various answers, is how to break the karmic chain so that one does not have to continue this dreary round of imperfect existences.

The enormous mass of Hindu scriptures is divided into two categories: *sruti*, "that which is heard," meaning that which was revealed to the ancient *rishis* or "seers" and, therefore, "that which rules authoritatively over mankind"; [5] and *smriti*, "that which is remembered," representing later scriptures whose insights go back to the *sruti*.

The *sruti*, therefore, is a primary authority. It consists of the *Veda*, meaning "wisdom" or "knowledge," and comprises the eternal word of truth heard intuitively by the seers or sages of the immemorial past. The Veda has evolved in three parts: the *Samhitas*, also called the Vedas—Rig-Veda, Yajur-Veda, Sama-Veda, and Artharva-Veda— which are very ancient collections of hymns and formulas for worship; the *Brahmanas*, or priestly and sacrificial texts; and the *Aranyakas*,

[5] V. Raghavan. "Introduction to the Hindu Scriptures." *The Religion of the Hindus*, ed. Kenneth W. Morgan (New York: The Ronald Press, 1953), p. 265.

or Forest Books, meditations from the seclusion of the forest, cul-
minating in the *Upanishads*, highly philosophical treatises centering
upon the nature of the eternal self within man and the eternal Self
within the universe.

The *smriti* is also authoritative but its authority is derivative from
the *sruti*. Though the Hindu classification of this voluminous and
diverse body of scripture is complex,[6] it can be subsumed under four
headings: [7] the *Sutras*, containing brief and pithy philosophic teachings, or aphorisms; the *Dharma Sastras*, or Law Books, composed
of Hindu legal codes, commentaries, and the like; the *Puranas*, recounting myths which extol certain of the principal Hindu deities;
and the two great epics, the *Mahabharata* and the *Ramayana*. Within
the *Mahabharata* is the shorter scripture called the *Bhagavad Gita*
or "Song of the Lord." The "Gita," as it is popularly called, sets
forth an impressive vision of the god Vishnu and nourishes the stream
of devotion in Hinduism in which God is worshiped as personal.
Though not ranking among the scriptures of primary authority *(sruti)*,
the Gita is undoubtedly the most influential and best loved single
scripture of Hinduism.

The structure and teaching of the Hindu scriptures is too complex
to be dealt with adequately here. Rather the major concern of this
discussion is the attitude toward or the doctrine of scripture in Hinduism. As in most religions, attitudes of Hindus toward their scriptures
vary. Some Hindu sectarian groups have their own scriptures (especially in the category of *smriti*) which interpret the older scriptures
according to their particular beliefs. There is the tendency to look
upon the Vedic scriptures *(sruti)* as infallible or verbally inspired.

Yet the view of revelation which underlies the attitude toward
scripture is very different from that of Christianity, Judaism, and Islam.
Revelation for Hinduism is not that which comes from personal
confrontation with the one God of the universe. Nor does it have
anything to do with a disclosure of God's character through historical
events. Rather, it is the eternal wisdom flowing from the springs of
the intuitive experience of the great seers of the past. This wisdom
is to be confirmed in the experience of the disciple.[8]

Cf. *ibid.*, pp. 269-74.

Cf. R. C. Zaehner, *Hinduism* (London: Oxford University Press, 1962), pp. 12-13.

M. Hiriyanna, *Essentials of Indian Philosophy* (London: George Allen and Unwin. Ltd., 1949),
p. 173.

The vast difference between this concept of revelation and that of Christianity is seen in the fact that atheistic schools of Indian philosophy, such as Purva Mimamsa, still believe strongly in revelation. Indeed, the Purva Mimamsa completely abolishes the idea of God—and yet adheres to the Veda as an infallible authority![9] In Hinduism, therefore, authoritative scriptures or "revealed truth," do not at all presuppose an Other who reveals. Instead truth is intuited from the very nature of reality. Revelation, then, is philosophical rather than historical.

This basic concept of "revealed" truth as illuminated intuition encourages tolerance. The Hindu is apt to acknowledge that the religious intuition of non-Hindus is also true—at least for them! Therefore, Hindus usually look upon other religions with respect and do not seek to convert their adherents to Hinduism. Rather, they tend to seek to include and absorb other religious practices and beliefs and thus to supplement the total store of intuitive truth.

Scriptures of Buddhism

Buddhism is a daughter of Hinduism; but, unlike the mother religion, Buddhism was missionary in spirit and spread widely to become the predominant religion of most of Asia east of India.

The founder of Buddhism was a man named Siddhartha Gautama, who lived in North India nearly six hundred years before Christ. He was later called "Buddha" or "Enlightened One" to indicate his experience of illumination. According to tradition, Gautama was reared in luxurious circumstances, the son of a king. However, he became impressed with the misery of human existence so that at the age of twenty-nine he left his affluent situation and his apparently ideal marital life to seek the answer to the problem of human suffering. His quest was essentially that of Hinduism: how to break the endless karmic chain of imperfect existences and find peace and fulfillment.

After unsuccessfully trying various methods recommended by Indian holy men, including extreme asceticism, the experience of enlightenment came to Gautama as he sat meditating beneath a tree. Salvation, he perceived, was to be gained by a middle way between self-mortification and self-indulgence. This middle way involved "Four Noble Truths" which came to Buddha in his enlightenment: (1) suffering is the universal human experience; (2) the cause of suffering is desire; (3) the way to end suffering is to extinguish desire; and (4) the way to extinguish desire and thus be rid of suffering is to follow the "Noble Eightfold Path" of right view, right aspiration, right speech, right action, right livelihood, right effort, right mindfulness, and right concentration, each step being carefully interpreted in terms of ethical and mental discipline.

The Eightfold Path, rightly followed, leads to the experience of Nirvana, a state in which all desire is extinguished and an indefinable bliss beyond ordinary consciousness is attained. For one who has experienced Nirvana all craving is gone, the impermanence of the self is recognized, and there is nothing about him to be born again, live again, or die again. Hence the chain of rebirths due to karma is broken.

The religion thus formed retained much from Hinduism but with new and specific interpretations. Also, it rejected certain items of Hindu belief, such as the caste system. Orders for monks and laymen were formed, and finally nunneries as well. Eventually, two great branches of Buddhism developed from Gautama's teaching. Southern Buddhism, known as Hinayana or Theravada, is conservative and tries to retain original Buddhism as unchanged as possible. It believes in no deities, though no doubt some of the common people look upon Buddha himself as a god. Southern Buddhism is found principally in Ceylon, Burma, Thailand, Cambodia, and Laos. Northern Buddhism, or Mahayana, has been much more open to non-Buddhist religious influences. It emphasizes some mythical Buddha figures, which serve as savior gods for the common people and as symbols of the ineffable Buddha reality for the sophisticated. Mahayana predominates in Vietnam, Tibet, China, Korea, and Japan. It is divided into many denominations or sects.

Within about five or six centuries the canon of Buddhist scriptures took shape. This canon was composed of what was judged to be the teachings of the Buddha and commentaries thereupon. These circulated in oral form, preserved by the memories of faithful monks, until the Fourth Great Buddhist Council, about 25 B.C., at which time they were written down in the ancient Indian language called "Pali." It is said that these Pali scriptures, if translated into English in their entirety, would fill more than a dozen large volumes.[10]

[10] U. Thittila. "The Fundamental Principles of Theravada Buddhism." *The Path of the Buddha*. ed. Kenneth W. Morgan (New York: The Ronald Press. 1956). p. 68.

These original scriptures of Buddhism are divided into three parts and are called *Tipitaka,* which means "Three Baskets." These three are *Vinaya Pitaka,* "The Basket of Discipline"; *Sutta Pitaka,* "The Basket of Discourses"; and *Abhidhamma Pitaka,* "The Basket of Ultimate Things" (or "The Basket of Philosophy"). The Basket of Discipline deals primarily with rules and regulations for the monks and nuns and is not very interesting to the general reader. However, it includes also an account of the life and ministry of the Buddha and the development of the Buddhist monastic order. The Basket of Discourses somewhat corresponds to the four Christian Gospels in that it gives the teaching and deeds of the Buddha, though it is written in much greater detail than the Gospels. The Basket of Ultimate Things is a highly philosophical treatment of the Buddhist system of thought, very technical, repetitious, and difficult to understand without considerable knowledge of Buddhism.[11]

The Pali Tipitaka just described is the canon of Southern or Theravada Buddhism. This canon, in the ancient Indian language known as Sanskrit, is incorporated into the Mahayana canon (Northern Buddhism), and has been translated into some of the other Asian languages, such as Chinese. However, the different Mahayana denominations have their own additional scriptures or *Sutras* which are generally regarded as more authoritative than the Tipitaka.[12]

There is, therefore, no one canon of scripture acceptable to all Buddhists. There is nothing like the unanimity as to canon which we know in Christianity where the only serious problem is the status of the Apocrypha. However, most Buddhists accept the scriptures of their own canon as the supreme source of knowledge and the authoritative standard for judgments of truth. An exception is the Zen sect, which emphasizes the direct apprehension of truth by meditation and intuitive insight. In some instances the scriptures are viewed by Buddhists in ways reminiscent of primitive magic. In Tibet, for example, the scriptures have their place in the Buddhist shrine as an object of worship. In the Nichiren sect—and its modern expression, the Soka Gakkai—the sect's authoritative scripture, the Lotus Sutra, is represented by a mandala or scroll on which the whole of transcendent

[11] *Ibid.,* pp. 68-70.
[12] Hajime Nakamura, "Unity and Diversity in Buddhism," *The Path of the Buddha,* ed. Kenneth W. Morgan (New York: The Ronald Press, 1956), pp. 390-92.

Buddha reality is represented by the Chinese characters of the names of the mythical Buddha personages or deities. To repeat the name of the Lotus Sutra with proper reverence is believed to assure one of blessings.

On the whole, however, the basic nature of the Buddhist scriptures is akin to that of the Hindu scriptures. The concept of revelation underlying the scriptures is intuitional. It is assumed that there is a world of transcendent, spiritual reality available to the intuition of the purified mind. While in Hinduism this reality is known through the diverse, seemingly contradictory insights of the sages, in Buddhism it is apprehended clearly by one Sage, Gautama Buddha. His followers find it by the Middle Way which he pointed out, and that way is set forth in the scriptures. Others find the Way as it is understood by their own Buddhist denomination and their respective scriptures, but it is related, however remotely, to the historical Buddha and his apprehensions of truth.

Thus, in Buddhism, the diversity of Hinduism comes to focus in one sage and one way, though Mahayana Buddhism reintroduces considerable diversity. There is possibility in Buddhism of a much more clearly defined central core of doctrine than is the case in Hinduism. What is more important, no doubt, is that the Buddha is a common symbol for the Buddhist faith in all its diversity, and this Buddha symbol is somehow related to the historical Gautama.

Nevertheless, in Buddhism, as in Hinduism, there is certainly no eternal Other who acts in history for man's redemption, who confronts man with a personal and sovereign claim. Scripture for Buddhism, therefore, cannot be the record of redemptive revelation in history coming to its crown and climax in one in whose face "we see the light of the knowledge of the glory of God." Rather, the monk must be a light to himself or, at most, he must find the teaching of the Buddha in the scriptures to be his light.

Scriptures of Islam

The Christian of Western background is apt to find himself on much more familiar ground when he encounters Islam or its Bible, the Koran, than when he is in touch with Hinduism or Buddhism. Islam, like Christianity and Judaism, originated in the Near East and among Semitic people. It is strongly monotheistic and emphasizes a unique revelation from the one God. It shares much of the Old

Testament history and claims Abraham as its great patriarch. Moreover, it reveals certain Christian influences. In fact, in its early history Islam was viewed by Christians as a Christian heresy.

The word "islam" means "submission"; "Moslem" means "one who submits." So Islam is the religion of submission to God. This religion embraces over four hundred million people distributed over a vast area from Africa to the Far East.

Non-Moslems usually consider the prophet Mohammed, who was born in Mecca, Arabia, in A.D. 571, as the founder of Islam and as the author of its sacred book, the Koran. Moslems, however, prefer to call him God's Messenger and the interpreter and exemplar of the Koran which they believe to be eternal.

In any case, Islam as an historical movement began with the preaching of Mohammed in the early part of the seventh century. Mohammed's preaching was based on experiences in which he believed that the angel Gabriel addressed him, declaring him to be God's messenger and giving him the words of his message. The Moslem calendar dates from A.D. 622, the year of Mohammed's flight (called the "Hegira") from Mecca to the nearby city of Medina because of persecution. Mohammed assumed the religious and political leadership of Medina, organized an army, and finally conquered Mecca in A.D. 630. Two years later he died, but his movement spread by military power and religious appeal. Within two or three centuries it spread over a vast empire stretching from Spain and North Africa in the west and to India in the east.

Moslem theology is relatively simple. The fundamental belief is in the one God, Allah, whose nature is absolutely undivided or unitary, not trinitarian. To the Moslem, the supreme sin is "associating" some other being with God as sharing his godhead or deity. The Christian doctrine of the Trinity comes under this negative judgment, and Christians are accused of worshipping three gods. The Moslems believe that God is absolutely transcendent and different from man so that an "incarnation" is unthinkable. Even to Mohammed, God did not reveal himself directly but through an angel. In the Koran, God's will is disclosed but not his essential nature, which is unknowable. The divine will is sovereign over all; therefore, Moslems believe in predestination without too much concern about the problem of its relation to human freedom.

A second important article of Moslem faith is the belief in prophets or apostles, of whom Mohammed is chief. Moslems recognize many of the biblical prophets from Noah to Jesus, but to them Mohammed is the "Seal of the Prophets" to whom the complete and final revelation has been given. Thus the Moslem "Word of Witness" declares that "There is no God but Allah and Mohammed is his Prophet." Though Mohammed is accorded great honor and respect, he is yet human; he is not considered divine.

Belief in the scriptures is also a basic belief of Moslems. As Mohammed is the final apostle or prophet, so the Koran is the final and complete scripture.

The Koran is very different from the Hindu and Buddhist scriptures; indeed it is unique among the scriptures of major religions for two or three reasons: (1) the Koran is definitely a "one man book." It contains only the alleged revelation of Allah to Mohammed. (2) The Koran gives no direct information at all about Mohammed and practically none about his companions or successors. For such knowledge one must depend on the extra-Koranic traditions. The name of Mohammed very rarely appears, and the revelations are introduced simply by the word "Say," roughly equivalent to the biblical "Thus saith the Lord." (3) The Koran was written down in its definitive form more quickly after Mohammed's death than were the sacred scriptures of other religions after the passing of their founders.[13]

The Koran is one volume, not very large, composed of one hundred and fourteen chapters or *Suras* of unequal length. Every Sura except one begins with the words "In the name of Allah, the Beneficent, the Merciful." Many of the Suras, especially the earlier ones, reveal not only the religious devotion but also the poetic genius of Mohammed, a particularly remarkable fact in view of the fact that he was illiterate. The Koran in the Arabic language is said to have an impressive poetic quality. Many of the later Suras, however, deal with detailed rules for the ordering of the Moslem state and definitely reflect the social structure and ideals of the Arabian society of Mohammed's day.[14]

Many familiar Old Testament characters reappear on the pages of the Koran, as do also Mary and Jesus. Since the Koran not only denounces the Christian doctrine of the Trinity but also makes several references to Jesus which do not agree with the New Testament

[13] Braden. *op. cit.*, pp. 439-40.
[14] *Ibid.*, pp. 446-50.

teaching, the Moslem almost inevitably believes that Christians are mistaken about the central figure of their faith. The Koran affirms the virgin birth of Jesus but strongly rejects his divine sonship. It refers to the future coming of Jesus but denies his crucifixion. Like Mohammed, Jesus is one of the prophets; but unlike Mohammed, he is not the "Seal of the Prophets."

The Moslem belief in scripture is the most emphatic possible. The Moslem is supposed to believe in all previous scriptures, but only insofar as these contained important truths for their day which were included perfectly and completely in the Koran. That is, the Moslem claims that by believing in the Koran he is actually believing in whatever was valid of all previous revelations. Though some Moslems are adopting a liberal attitude toward the actual language of the Koran, and by implication, many of its ideas, they nevertheless affirm its authority and its central message.[15]

More characteristic than liberal views, however, are the exalted and emphatic claims for the infallibility and perfection of the Koran. For example, an authoritative interpreter of Islamic faith, a professor of the interpretation of the Koran at Al Azhdr University, Cairo, Egypt, declares that the Koran is "a miracle—yes, rather THE miracle," and that everything concerning the Koran proves its supernatural character.[16] He summarizes a discussion of the Koran by calling it "a purely divine work . . . the Word of God . . . perfection itself . . . unchallengeably true, infallibly just, and inimitably good and beautiful." [17]

Just as Christians traditionally believe Christ existed from all eternity, so Moslems traditionally believe the Koran is uncreated and eternally inscribed in heaven. Therefore, the real revelational parallel between Christianity and Islam is not that of Bible and Koran but that of Christ and Koran. From the Christian standpoint, revelation is not primarily the Bible itself but God's free, sovereign, and continuous action in history. To this the Bible witnesses, culminating in God's revelation in Jesus of Nazareth, who is the central focus of the biblical witness and the supremely authoritative disclosure of the revealing

[15] Cf. Asaf A. A. Fyzee. *A Modern Approach to Islam* (Bombay: Asia Publishing House, 1963), pp. 93-94.

[16] Mohammad Abd Allah Draz. "The Origin of Islam." *Islam—The Straight Path*, ed. Kenneth W. Morgan (New York: The Ronald Press, 1958), p. 16.

[17] *Ibid.*, p. 40.

God. On the other hand, from the standpoint of the Koran, revelation is supremely the Koran itself, the immutable, inerrant, infallible words of the book. Hendrik Kraemer stated the contrast succinctly: "The foundation of Islam is not, The Word became flesh. It is, The Word became book." [18]

Conclusion

Early in this chapter the sacred Scriptures were distinguished from other literature. It is now appropriate to ask in what way the Christian Bible is to be distinguished from the scriptures of other religions.

The uniqueness of the Bible among other "Bibles" does not inhere in its "religious" character. Other scriptures are also religious, that is, they have to do with God or spiritual reality, worship, religious duties, etc. Nor does the Bible's uniqueness consist in the claim to a verbally infallible revelation in a book. No Christian can outdo the Moslems in this claim.

In part, the Bible's uniqueness is to be found in the historical character of the revelation to which it testifies. It traces the course of God's revealing and redeeming work in history for all men through a people who understood themselves in a singular sense as God's people. But even this feature is true in some measure of the Koran and is certainly true of the Jewish Bible apart from the New Testament.

In the deeper sense, the uniqueness of the Christian Bible inheres in the uniqueness of the Christ to whom it witnesses. Jesus Christ himself is the great "Revealing Act" [19] of God. The Bible points to him as the Fulfiller of the Old Covenant (Testament) and as the Lord and initiator of the New Covenant (Testament), the new age, and the new creation. Within and beyond the sacred page he stands and confronts us with a sovereign claim: "I am the way, and the truth, and the life; no one comes to the Father, but by me" (John 14:6, RSV).

[18] Hendrik Kraemer, *The Christian Message in a Non-Christian World* (New York: Harper and Brothers, 1938), pp. 217-18.

[19] Bouquet, *op. cit.*, p. 114.

Bibliography

CHAPTER ONE

NIDA, EUGENE A. *God's Word in Man's Language.* New York: Harper and Brothers, 1952.

PHILLIPS, J. B. *Ring of Truth.* New York: The Macmillan Company, 1967.

CHAPTER THREE

HERRING, RALPH A. *God Being My Helper.* Nashville: Broadman Press, 1955.

TOZER, A. W. *The Divine Conquest.* Harrisburg, Penn.: Christian Publications, Inc. 1950.

CHAPTER FOUR

BLACK, MATTHEW AND ROWLEY, H. H. eds. *Peake's Commentary on the Bible.* New York: Thomas Nelson, Inc. 1962.

BUTTRICK, GEORGE A., ed. *The Interpreter's Dictionary of the Bible.* Nashville: Abingdon Press, 1962.

DANA, H. E. AND GLAZE, R. E. *Interpreting the New Testament.* Nashville: Broadman Press, 1961.

DANKER, FREDERICK W. *Multipurpose Tools for Bible Study.* St. Louis: Concordia Publishing House, 1960.

ELLISON, JOHN W., ed. *Nelson's Complete Concordance of the Revised Standard Version of the Bible.* New York: Thomas Nelson, Inc., 1957.

GOETCHIUS, EUGENE VAN NESS. *The Language of the New Testament.* New York: Scribner's, 1965.

GROBEL, K. "History and Principles of Interpretation," *The Interpreter's Dictionary of the Bible,* II.

MOWRY, L. "Allegory," *The Interpreter's Dictionary of the Bible,* I.

STAGG, FRANK. *New Testament Theology.* Nashville: Broadman Press, 1962.

STRONG, JAMES. *Exhaustive Concordance of the Bible,* 26th printing. Nashville: Abingdon Press, 1965.

YOUNG, ROBERT. *Young's Analytical Concordance to the Bible,* rev. ed. Grand Rapids: Wm. B. Eerdman's, 1955.

CHAPTER SEVEN

JONES, ALEXANDER. *The Jerusalem Bible.* New York: Doubleday, 1967.

MOULTON, RICHARD. *The Modern Reader's Bible.* London: The Macmillan Co., 1912.

CHAPTER EIGHT

COLWELL, E. C. *The Study of the Bible.* Chicago: University of Chicago Press, 1937.

FILSON, FLOYD V. *Which Books Belong in the Bible?* Philadelphia: The Westminster Press, 1957.

GOODSPEED, E. J. *How Came the Bible?* Nashville: Abingdon Press, 1940.

GRANT, ROBERT M. *The Formation of the New Testament.* New York: Harper and Row, 1965.

KENYON, SIR FREDERIC. *The Story of the Bible,* reprinted, London: John Murray, 1944.

ORLINSHY, H. M. "Genizah," *The Interpreter's Dictionary of the Bible,* II.

PFEIFFER, R. H. "Canon of the Old Testament," *The Interpreter's Dictionary of the Bible,* IV.

PRUSSNER, FREDERICK C. "Problems Ahead in Old Testament Research," *The Study of the Bible Today and Tomorrow.* Chicago: University of Chicago Press, 1947.

ROBERTS, B. J. "Old Testament Text," *The Interpreter's Dictionary of the Bible,* IV.

ROBERTS, B. J. "The Ancient Versions of the Old Testament," *Peake's Commentary on the Bible.*

WEVERS, J. W. "Septuagint," *The Interpreter's Dictionary of the Bible,* IV.

CHAPTER NINE

METZGER, BRUCE M. *The Text of the New Testament.* New York: Oxford University Press, 1964.

PARVIS, M. M. "New Testament Text," *The Interpreter's Dictionary of the Bible,* IV.

CHAPTER TEN

BLACK, MATTHEW. *An Aramaic Approach to the Gospels and Acts,* 2nd ed. Oxford: Clarendon Press, 1954.

BURKITT, F. C. *Gospel History and Its Transmission,* Edinburgh: T. & T. Clark, 1907.

BUTLER, B. C. *The Originality of St. Matthew.* Cambridge: The University Press, 1951.

CREED, J. M. *The Gospel According to St. Luke.* London: The Macmillan Co., 1930.

DUPONT, JACQUES. *The Sources of Acts*, tr. by Kathleen Pond. London: Darton, Longman and Todd, 1964.

Encyclopedia Britannica

FARMER, W. R. *The Synoptic Gospels.* New York: The Macmillan Co., 1964.

FREEDMAN, D. N. "Pentateuch," *The Interpreter's Dictionary of the Bible*, III.

GROBEL, K. "Biblical Criticism," *The Interpreter's Dictionary of the Bible*, I.

———. "Form Criticism," *The Interpreter's Dictionary of the Bible*, II.

HARNACK, A. *Luke the Physician*, tr. by J. R. Wilkinson. New York: G. P. Putnam's Sons, 1907.

———. *The Acts of the Apostles*, tr. by J. R. Wilkinson. New York: G. P. Putnam's Sons, 1909.

KNOX, JOHN. *Jesus, Lord and Christ.* Reissued; Harper and Row, 1958.

MORTON, A. Q. AND MACGREGOR, G. H. C. *The Structure of Luke and Acts.* New York: Harper and Row, 1964.

NEILL, STEPHEN. *The Interpretation of the New Testament, 1861-1961.* New York: Oxford University Press, 1964.

NIELSON, EDUARD. "Studies in Biblical Theology No. 11," *Oral Tradition.* Chicago: Alec R. Allenson, 1954.

PARKER, PIERSON. *The Gospel Before Mark.* Greenwich, Conn.: Seabury Press, 1953.

ROBERTSON, A. T. *A Harmony of the Gospels for Students of the Life of Christ.* New York: Harper and Brothers, 1922.

STREETER, B. H. *The Four Gospels*, 5th impression. New York: St. Martin's Press, 1964.

TAYLOR, VINCENT. *Behind the Third Gospel.* Oxford: Clarendon Press, 1926.

WILLIAMS, C. S. C. "The Synoptic Problem," *Peake's Commentary on the Bible.*

WILSON, J. Christy. *Introducing Islam.* New York: Friendship Press, 1959.

CHAPTER ELEVEN

BLACK, M. H. "The Printed Bible," *The Cambridge History of the Bible*, ed. by S. L. Greenslade. Cambridge University Press, 1963.

BRUCE, F. F. *The English Bible.* New York: Oxford University Press, 1961.

GRANT, F. C. *Translating the Bible.* Greenwich, Conn.: Seabury Press, 1961.

WIKGREN, A. "The English Versions of the Bible," *Peake's Commentary on the Bible.*

CHAPTER TWELVE

MOULTON, JAMES H. AND MILLIGAN, GEORGE. *The Vocabulary of the Greek Testament.* London: Hodder and Stoughton, 1930.

APPENDIX

BALLOU, ROBERT O. *The Bible of the World.* New York: Viking Press, 1939.

BOUQUET, A. C. *The Christian Faith and Non-Christian Religions.* New York: Harper and Brothers, 1958.

BRADEN, CHARLES S. *The Scriptures of Mankind.* New York: The Macmillan Co., 1952.

DRAZ, MOHAMMAD ABD ALLAH. "The Origin of Islam," *Islam—The Straight Path,* ed. Kenneth W. Morgan. New York: The Ronald Press, 1958.

FYZEE, ASAF A. A. *A Modern Approach to Islam.* Bombay: Asia Publishing House, 1963.

HIRIYANNA, M. *Essentials of Indian Philosophy.* London: George Allen Unwin, Ltd., 1949.

————. *Outlines of Indian Philosophy.* London: George Allen and Unwin, Ltd., 1932.

KRAEMER, HENDRIK. *The Christian Message in a Non-Christian World.* New York: Harper and Brothers, 1938.

NAKAMURA, HAJIME. "Unity and Diversity in Buddhism," *The Path of the Buddha,* ed. by Kenneth W. Morgan. New York: The Ronald Press, 1956.

RAGHAVAN, V. "Introduction to the Hindu Scriptures," *The Religion of the Hindus,* ed. by Kenneth W. Morgan. New York: The Ronald Press, 1953.

THITTILA, U. "The Fundamental Principles of Theravada Buddhism," *The Path of the Buddha,* ed. by Kenneth W. Morgan. New York: The Ronald Press, 1956.

ZAEHNER, R. C. *Hinduism.* London: Oxford University Press, 1962.

About the Authors

E. Luther Copeland is professor of missions at Southeastern Baptist Seminary. Born in West Virginia, he was pastor of churches in North Carolina, Indiana, and Connecticut. He studied at Mars Hill College; Furman University (B.A.); Furman University (B.A.); University of Kentucky; Southern Baptist Seminary (Th.M.); Yale University (Ph.D.); and Banaras Hindu University, Banaras, India. Dr. Copeland is a well-known author and lecturer in the field of missions.

Ralph A. Herring was a pastor for thirty-eight years, twenty-five of these as pastor of the First Baptist Church, Winston-Salem, North Carolina. Having served as director of the Seminary Extension Department of Southern Baptist Seminaries for seven years, he retired to devote his time to writing, preaching, and Bible teaching. Born in North Carolina of missionary parents, he spent his boyhood in China. He studied at Wake Forest College (B.A.) and at the Southern Baptist Theological Seminary (Th.M., Ph.D.).

James Wesley Ingles was born in Scotland. He studied at Wheaton College (B.A.), Princeton Theological Seminary (Th.B.), Princeton University (M.A.), Eastern Baptist Theological Seminary (D.D.), and Drew University. He is a well-known teacher and pastor in addition to being an author of five novels, a short story writer, and a contributing editor of *Christianity Today*. Dr. Ingles retired as head of the English Department of Eastern Baptist College in 1968 to devote full time to writing.

John P. Newport, a native of Missouri, is professor of philosophy and religion at Southwestern Baptist Theological Seminary. He studied at William Jewell College (B.A.); Southern Baptist Seminary (Th.M., Th.D); Texas Christian University (M.A.); University of Edinburgh, Scotland (Ph.D.); the universities of Basel and of Zurich, Switzerland; Tulane University; and the University of Tulsa. Dr. Newport served pastorates in four states and was professor at Baylor University and New Orleans Baptist Seminary before going to Southwestern Seminary. He is a popular speaker, especially for youth groups at home and abroad.

Eugene A. Nida is executive secretary for the Translations Department of the American Bible Society. His work has taken him to more than seventy countries, where he has conferred with translators on linguistic problems involving more than 150 different languages. He is a native of Oklahoma and studied at the University of California at Los Angeles (B.A.), the University of Southern California (M.A.), and the University of Michigan (Ph.D.). For sixteen years he was professor of linguistics at the Summer Institute of Linguistics, University of Oklahoma. Dr. Nida is a prolific writer and is the recipient of the 1967 Gutenberg Award presented by the Chicago Bible Society for distinguished service in the cause of Scripture distribution.

Frank Stagg is professor of New Testament at the Southern Baptist Theological Seminary. A native of Louisiana, he pastored a church in Louisiana and taught at the New Orleans Baptist Theological Seminary before going to Southern Seminary. He studied at Louisiana College (B.A.); Southern Baptist Seminary (Th.M., Ph.D.); Union Theological Seminary; University of Edinburgh, Scotland; University of Basel, Switzerland; and University of Tuebingen, Germany. Dr. Stagg is a noted author and lecturer.